THE INTERNATIONAL MEGALOPOLIS

The International Megalopolis

Edited by

MASON WADE

The Eighth Annual
University of Windsor Seminar on
Canadian-American Relations

PUBLISHED FOR THE UNIVERSITY OF WINDSOR
BY UNIVERSITY OF TORONTO PRESS

IN MEMORIAM
The Rev. Frank J. Boland, CSB
(1917–1969)
Director of the Canadian-American Seminars
1959–1967

Contents

Contributors

WALTER H. BLUCHER, Planning Consultant, Arlington, Vermont

MARION CLAWSON, Director, Land Use and Management Program, Resources for the future, Washington, DC

ANTHONY DOWNS, Senior Economic Analyst and Senior Vice-President, Real Estate Research Corporation, Chicago, Illinois

C. A. DOXIADIS, President of Doxiadis Associates, Consultants on Development of Ekistics, and Chairman, Board of Directors, Athens Technological Institute, Athens, Greece

MARVIN B. FAST, Program Operations Officer, Great Lakes Laboratory, Ann Arbor, Michigan

HERB GRAY, Member of Parliament, Essex West

J. P. HARTT, Professor, Department of Civil Engineering, University of Windsor, Windsor, Ontario

HARLAN H. HATCHER, President, University of Michigan, Ann Arbor, Michigan

G. R. HEFFERNAN, President, Lake Ontario Steel Co. Ltd., Whitby, Ontario

MAURICE F. PARKINS, President, Parkins, Rogers and Associates, Planning and Urban Renewal Consultants, Detroit, Michigan

E. G. PLEVA, Chairman, Department of Geography, University of Western Ontario, London, Ontario

JACK C. RANSOME, Chairman, Department of Geography, University of Windsor, Windsor, Ontario

RONALD S. RITCHIE, Director, Imperial Oil Ltd.

JOHN ROBARTS, Prime Minister of the Province of Ontario

E. A. G. ROBINSON, Secretary, Royal Economic Society, Cambridge, England

O. M. SOLANDT, Vice-President, Research and Development, de Haviland Aircraft of Canada, Ltd., and Chancellor, University of Toronto, Toronto, Ontario

D. M. STEPHENS, Chairman, Manitoba Hydro, and Member, Canadian Section, International Joint Commission

Introduction

THE WORLD POPULATION EXPLOSION is a reflection of urban growth. No part of the world has escaped the pressures built up by expanding cities. In some areas cities are growing towards each other and will eventually join together in continuous urban landscapes. No planned shape takes form on the regional scale: subdivisions, industrial districts, towns, and villages are drawn into something that has an identity, a reality, and a character defying precise definitions. A megalopolis is the most amorphous of urban entities. It may cover hundreds of square miles, spilling into several states or provinces. Jean Gottmann has attempted to define the seaboard megalopolis of North America in a descriptive interpretation. Constantin Doxiadis, on the other hand, in attempting to define the Great Lakes megalopolis of North America, starts with description but goes on to analysis, interpretation, and planning.

The automobile, as the preferred form of mechanical, personal transportation, is determining the shape of the modern city. It is appropriate that the Detroit region, the heart of the automobile industry in North America, should be the first urban area to be studied thoroughly from the circulation and mobility point of view. Although land uses may seem to be focused on specific parcels of land, these uses change in relation to the influences of other uses in the urban complex. The mechanism of influence is the circulatory system of roadways, railways, pipelines, airways, and electrical networks. Doxiadis interprets present and future land use patterns in the context of existing and developing circulatory arrangements.

The greatest problem facing urban man is related to his power and ability to channel the burgeoning urban growth into productive, compatible, and beautiful patterns. With this in mind, the University of Windsor chose "The Great Lakes Megalopolis" as its 1966 seminar topic.

Doxiadis Associates, at the request of the Detroit Edison Company, started a five-year study in January 1965 on the emergence and growth of the Detroit urban region. The first of three volumes, published in time for the 1966 seminar, is an overall analysis of the developing Detroit area. The second volume, published in 1967, deals with future alternatives. The third volume, to be published in 1970, will deal with interpretation as a broad basis for planning.

The Detroit study served as a keynote to the seminar. Problems of urban growth were discussed against the solid backdrop of the detailed study of the home region. The invited papers were on general, universal, and perhaps even eclectic urban problems; yet the discussions and examples were specific when seen on the regional scale of Detroit whose downtown skyline is clearly visible from the campus of the University of Windsor. Thus the Doxiadis report on Detroit provided the focal point for the discussions.

By the second day it was evident that four major topics were being discussed in both structured and unstructured ways: (*a*) fragmentation of the administrative urban region, (*b*) the fitness of the urban environment, (*c*) the special planning problems of the Great Lakes drainage basin, and (*d*) the concept of an evolving civilized urban landscape.

North America was settled by Europeans who brought

their institutions to a new continent. Over the years these institutions changed slowly as problem-solving challenges were faced. The local forms of government brought largely from England have not, strangely enough, changed as rapidly as in their country of origin. The town, township, and county pattern of local government served our agrarian past very well. However, in metropolitan areas and specifically in the megalopolis, these inherited forms of local government are not suitable for dealing with important regional problems.

A great change has taken place in man's living space in urban America – a change due mainly to the impact of the automobile on the shape of cities. Today's citizen does not know where he lives in relation to the tidy units of local government his grandfather knew. In a single day, he may include in his effective living space as many as twelve different units of local government. This space, simply stated, has grown far beyond the limits set by the boundaries of local government.

The seminar explored ways whereby regional thinking could be carried out effectively in a fragmented administrative mosaic. Many solutions were suggested, all of which would require information such as that put together by the Doxiadis team.

A large part of the seminar's time was concerned with environmental planning. Civilized men, or at least those who aspire to be civilized, are trying to determine the bounds of adaptability in the human condition so that they may enjoy the physical resources of the environment without lessening or destroying the resource base. To what extent can the environment be altered without peril to human survival?

Mastery of the environment is almost exclusively adaptive. Modern urban concentration is a testimony to adaptive skills: the conditioning of climate, clothing to provide a personal microclimate, a diet gathered all over the world and available in and out of season, mechanical (usually personal) transportation to move people around, a communicating language reinforced by communication machinery, and a division of labour to facilitate specialization.

Urban man keeps asking himself the question, "Is what is happening leading to some kind of optimal environment?" There are increasing doubts that bigness alone will lead to a better urban condition. In fact, there is a strong opinion that many urban areas have passed an optimum scale in such things as housing, urban design, transportation systems, air and water standards, and allocation of land uses.

Is there a kind of balance in the urban condition? Many who have looked at this question think that the so-called balance is a razor's edge where the slightest aberration has irreversible consequences. This concept is too simple. On the other hand, neither is this balance a log-jam where only excessive charges of dynamite are effective. In every urban relationship the true condition is somewhere in between. The study of the Detroit region showed the seminar that the tolerable bounds in thousands of complicated urban relationships can be understood and used in planning only after the fullest information, systematically assembled, is made available to those who must make decisions and then act on them.

The Detroit region is geographically the pivot point of the entire Great Lakes system. The Great Lakes megalopolis is one of the world's most important industrial and urban areas, with a rate of development which now equals and in the next decade will exceed that of other urban areas, including the Eastern megalopolis. One of the major assets of the Great Lakes megalopolis is the Great Lakes system itself.

The physical map of North America shows a natural unity in the Great Lakes–St. Lawrence drainage basin: it is one system. However, the political map displays a pattern of fragmentation. The natural unit is shared by two countries, nine states and two provinces, and over ten thousand units of local government. How does one arrive at an orderly comprehensive scheme for the solving of problems that are regional in scale? In the Detroit area studied by Doxiadis, over seven hundred "jurisdictions," each with both specific and general obligations or responsibilities, make regional approaches to regional problems difficult.

The seminar did not produce many proposals as to ways in which a large urban region in the Great Lakes drainage basin may be administered, but a number of suggestions were put forth as to the ways in which the problem could be studied. The Detroit region is particularly interesting as a study area because it involves the challenge of an international situation. The model to be used in the Detroit area would have many useful applications in a world struggling to evolve mechanisms for international co-operation.

Perhaps the most optimistic outcome of the seminar dealt with a general appreciation of what could be called the evolution of a civilized landscape. There are many legitimate land uses: space for houses, industries, water supply, roads, hospitals, shopping centres, cemeteries, parks, schools, farms, mines and quarries, grazing land, docks, television towers, canals, airports, forests, electrical energy installations, hotels, libraries, theatres, recreational areas, wilderness, scenic vistas, sewers and sewage disposal systems, and at least a score of other major needs. All are legitimate, all are needed. The challenge of the civilized landscape is to see that each is put in its right place and that each does not detract from the maximum effectiveness of every other legitimate land use.

This challenge sounds terrifying, yet in the context of

an information system as carried out by Doxiadis Associates for the Detroit area it seems manageable.

The Detroit study is important for many reasons, but two major attributes of the Doxiadis approach had a profound effect on the discussions during and after the seminar: the significance of organizing information quantitatively so that the people who must make decisions can choose intelligently between alternatives, and the significance of looking at a large region in a unitary way so that the representatives of the small, fragmented units of local government may make decisions relevant to the total urban complex.

Whenever a decision or choice is made, there are countless numbers of non-choices that could have been made. What were the criteria for choice? The Doxiadis study is like a manual in decision-making. It is a kind of urban game in which roles may be taken by the players. The factual information is presented clearly in tables, text, and maps. Fortunately (or unfortunately, depending on one's point of view), urban development is more than a game. The simile, however, is apt. The variables are related to social and political organization as well as to the physical base. Often what seemed to be an excellent proposal could not be carried out because of constraints imposed by inherited cultural forms. It was obvious in the seminar discussions that the solutions for regional urban problems could not wait for the establishment of a centralized authority with centralized solutions. In fact, it was apparent that simplified central solutions often created special problems. The solution to regional urban problems on a regional scale rests primarily with the improvement of information systems, with evolving programs for regional development participated in by all the constituent members, and a complete understanding of the regional system of relationships by those agencies that operate on a regional basis. The Detroit Edison Company operates on a regional scale and, significantly, is probably the only agency that could support and produce a regional study treating the region as an entity and not merely as an assemblage of inherited postage-stamp-size administrative fragments.

Most of the time spent both formally and informally was centred on the ways and means of achieving regional understanding so that regional problems could be dealt with on a regional scale. It was taken as axiomatic that the outcomes of any sensible program of urban planning and development would be related to the usually stated objectives: (a) the developing and maintaining of continuously vigorous centres of industry, commerce, and culture, (b) the provision of good housing in good neighbourhoods, (c) efficient urban transportation to move goods and people easily about the entire urban region, (d) efficient regional energy systems of electricity, telecommunication, pipelines of water and fuel, and regional systems of waste treatment and pollution control, and (e) sufficient and appropriate financing for public and private improvement.

In the planning stages it was feared that the seminar might end up as just another conference in which the usual outcomes were debated another time. Fortunately, the Doxiadis study kept the subsequent discussions closely knit to the means by which the desirable outcomes of urban planning and development may be achieved.

E. G. PLEVA

THE INTERNATIONAL MEGALOPOLIS

THE INTERNATIONAL SCENE

1. THE PROSPECT OF
AN INTERNATIONAL MEGALOPOLIS*

C. A. DOXIADIS

INTRODUCTION

SEVERAL URBANIZED AREAS around the world deserve the title of megalopolis, at least as unified groupings of urban – mostly metropolitan – clusters interconnected by numerous ties in a kind of usually linear formation. This interconnectedness, however, is not to be understood as involving the continuity of the built-up area which may well be distributed in widely separated clusters within each such megalopolis. It is to be seen as a functional interconnectedness involving multiple ties of transportation, communication, economic and social links, and contacts, etc. In the light of such a preliminary definition of the megalopolitan concept, about ten megalopolises have been identified as being well under way around the world. Many more are anticipated by 1980, their number increasing sharply towards the end of the century when many tens of megalopolises are expected to be formed throughout the world according to a preliminary study undertaken within the framework of the "City of the Future" research project of

*A summary of the main address. Owing to the large number of slides used in the actual presentation, technical considerations make complete reproduction very difficult. For this reason, the summary presented is based on the relevant chapter devoted to the Great Lakes megalopolis appearing in *Emergence and Growth of an Urban Region, The Developing Urban Detroit Area, Volume 1: Analysis* (The Detroit Edison Co. 1966).

the Athens Center of Ekistics, reported in the July 1965 issue of *Ekistics*.

It is anticipated that one of the more important of these will develop in the Great Lakes area. Quite apart from the "City of the Future" research project and independently of each other, the current thinking of many authors and administrative authorities seems to take into account the possibility of the emergence of something like a Great Lakes megalopolis. A large proportion of the inhabitants of this area seems to feel that such a megalopolis is coming.

How far are we entitled to speak already of a Great Lakes megalopolis? So far there do not seem to be sufficiently detailed studies to give an answer to this problem. In the study of the urban Detroit area a preliminary examination was necessary to consider the extent of the megalopolitan characteristics evident in the Great Lakes area, as well as the position and relative importance of our study area within this major urban complex.

As a first approach, the study was oriented towards defining and identifying the area within which a megalopolis is thought to be emerging. Second, it attempted a comparison with the existing and more advanced megalopolitan development along the eastern seaboard of the United States (Eastern megalopolis) to determine whether the suspected Great Lakes megalopolis could be compared with the Eastern megalopolis at some earlier stage.

In view of the fact that one of the primary objectives was to define the area within which the Great Lakes megalopolis is supposed to be emerging, the method followed was to proceed by successive approximations based on the study of various phenomena by counties.

Three major clusters have been isolated as constituting the main elements of the US part of the Great Lakes megalopolis: one centred on Chicago, another on Detroit, and a third, with a double focal point, Cleveland–Pittsburgh. Also considered were the possibilities of a northeastern extension into Canada, as well as a connection with other adjacent urban clusters such as one around Cincinnati in the south, or a branch extending south of Lakes Erie and Ontario, east through the Mohawk Valley, and forming a link between the Great Lakes megalopolis and the Eastern megalopolis.

A comprehensive study of the megalopolis concept should take into account that it is inherent in a definition of megalopolis to consider it as growing through time so that the boundaries are constantly changing. This is well illustrated in Gottmann's "Megalopolis,"* where two different areas, one for 1950 and another larger one for 1960, are shown. Consequently, if a Great Lakes megalopolis were already in existence, it would have boundaries covering a larger area today than before, and would be expected to cover a still larger area in the future.

For purposes of comparison between the Eastern megalopolis and the assumed megalopolitan development around the Great Lakes, two constant areas were defined. For the Great Lakes megalopolis a preliminary definition was adopted (Fig. 1), while for the Eastern megalopolis the area considered was that defined by Gottmann in 1960.

The analysis of the Great Lakes megalopolis was presented through a series of maps showing the distribution of various phenomena in the area concerned. Many of these maps seem to delineate rather clearly an area surrounding the Great Lakes megalopolis separated by zones of different character from other regions. Smaller densities of population and the mountainous terrain of the Appalachian region

*J. Gottmann: *Megalopolis – The Urbanized North-eastern Seaboard of the United States.* A 20th Century Fund Study. Massachusetts Institute of Technology Press. 1961.

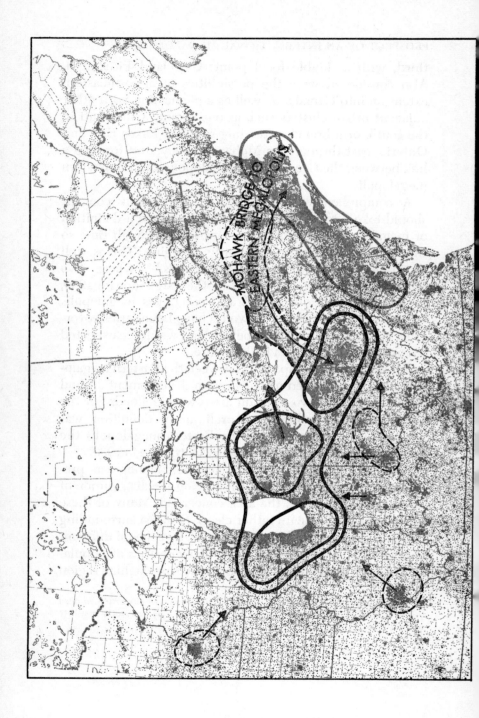

MOHAWK BRIDGE TO
EASTERN MEGALOPOLIS

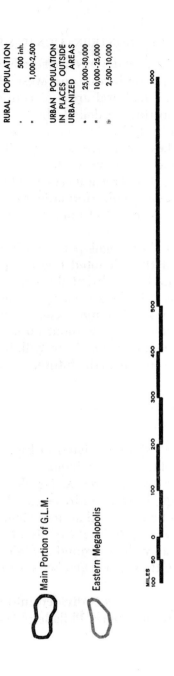

FIG. 1 A preliminary definition of the Great Lakes megalopolis.

divide the Great Lakes megalopolis from the Eastern megalopolis. To the south, southwest, and west of the Great Lakes megalopolis, agricultural areas of considerable importance seem to constitute a definite break between this area and other urbanized areas farther south or west. In the north, the Great Lakes themselves still constitute a rather marked natural boundary. However, to the north of Lakes Huron and Superior, the Precambrian shield of Canada and other geologic or geographic formations less favourable to urban developments seem to form a more realistic kind of northern barrier.

The terms Great Lakes megalopolis and Eastern megalopolis are used as if they denoted two comparable concepts. It should be understood that the term Great Lakes megalopolis is not used in the sense of proposing a proven magalopolis but merely as a more convenient term for defining the area under study, without implying whether this does already form a megalopolis or will, it is believed, constitute one at a given date in the future.

DESCRIPTIVE ANALYSIS OF
THE VARIOUS PHENOMENA

Urbanized areas in 1960 are depicted in Fig. 2, on which respective zones of influence are evident.

In the Great Lakes area, three major clusters are evident, around Chicago, Detroit, and Cleveland–Pittsburgh. Smaller clusters can be identified around Cincinnati–Dayton–Columbus, St. Louis, and Minneapolis–St. Paul, on the United States side, as well as around Buffalo–Hamilton–Toronto, Montreal–Ottawa, and Quebec on the Canadian extension.

The East Coast megalopolis is divided into three major clusters, Washington–Baltimore, Philadelphia–New York, and Providence–Boston.

Following the preliminary identification of the Great Lakes megalopolis, the relative degree of development of the two megalopolises on the basis of a number of variables is assessed.

The first variable selected was total urban population within the two megalopolises at different time periods. Such periods were so selected (among the various decennial statistics) as to give an analogous visual impression of the distribution of city sizes within the two megalopolitan areas, thus defining the time lag. The conclusion that can be drawn is that the time lag between the development of the Eastern and Great Lakes megalopolises is constantly decreasing.

Further analysis showed that in 1790 the populations size of the urban centres in the Eastern megalopolis was comparable to that of the Great Lakes in 1840. This fifty-year population gap narrowed to forty years later on in the nineteenth century (1810–30 for the Eastern megalopolis and 1850–70 for the Great Lakes megalopolis) to reach eventually a thirty-year time lag within the twentieth century, as shown in Fig. 3.

The thirty-year time lag refers to the period 1910–30 for the Eastern megalopolis and to 1940–60 for the Great Lakes megalopolis. The circles on Fig. 3 representing population show a very similar size distribution in both megalopolises. Within the Great Lakes megalopolis, the Chicago and Cleveland–Pittsburgh clusters are prominent, with Detroit following closely. The Cincinnati–Dayton and Buffalo–Toronto clusters are smaller but show a more rapid population increase. The Montreal–Ottawa cluster, still smaller, shows a moderate rate of increase.

The two megalopolises were compared for the same years by studying the evolution of densities by SMSA's (standard metropolitan statistical areas). In 1910 only the Chicago cluster was prominent in the Great Lakes, while on the east

URBANIZED AREAS
🌼 Extent of areas

RURAL POPULATION
.   500 inh.
•   1,000-2,500

URBAN POPULATION
IN PLACES OUTSIDE
URBANIZED AREAS
•   25,000-50,000
•   10,000-25,000
⊛   2,500-10,000

MILES
100 50 0   100   200   300   400   500   1000

FIG. 2   Urbanized area, 1960.

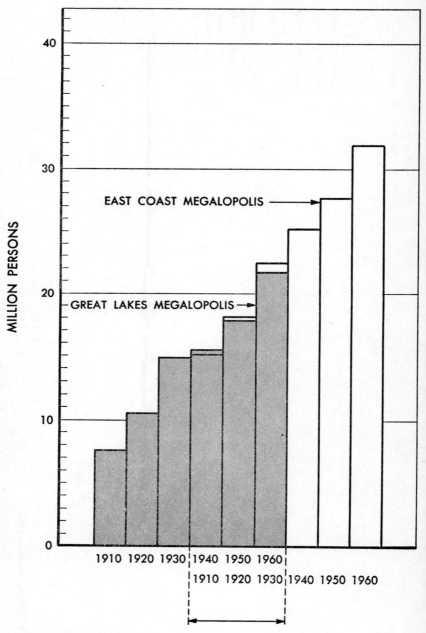

FIG. 3   Thirty-year time lag.

coast the three major clusters, Washington–Baltimore, Philadelphia–New York, and Providence–Boston were conspicuous. In 1930–50, the Detroit and Cleveland–Pittsburgh clusters are comparable to Chicago and the Washington–Baltimore, Providence–Boston clusters. The clusters of the Canadian extension of the Great Lakes megalopolis also begin to appear, as does the Mohawk "bridge."

By 1960 all major clusters of the Great Lakes megalopolis had attained population densities comparable with those of the eastern clusters.

Population trends by counties for the period 1940–60 are shown in Fig. 4. This figure shows a large area surrounding both the Great Lakes megalopolis and the Eastern megalopolis, and particularly the dividing line between the two along the Appalachian Mountains from West Virginia to the central part of Pennsylvania. It also delimits the Great Lakes megalopolis towards the south, southwest, and west from the adjacent less urbanized agricultural areas. The Great Lakes megalopolis is seen to extend southwest towards Peoria, Springfield, Terre Haute, Louisville. The broader region within which the Great Lakes megalopolis and the east coast megalopolis are likely to grow is clearly indicated.

Population change by counties for 1950–60 shows high rates of increase around the Chicago, Detroit, and Cleveland clusters. The Canadian side is quite prominent especially for the London–Hamilton–Toronto cluster and the Montreal cluster.

The Eastern megalopolis is indicated in its entirety, subdivided into the Washington–Baltimore cluster and the Philadelphia–New York cluster extending northward. It is characteristic that the centres of all major cities, New York, Boston, Chicago, etc., either decline or grow very slowly.

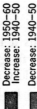

MILES
100 50   0   100   200   300   400   500   1000

FIG. 4 Population trends by counties, 1940–60.

The percentage of urban population to total population for all counties of the area concerned, including Canada, was one of the most important variables as an index of urbanization and megalopolitan maturity.

Family-income distribution showed the percentage of families earning over $5,000 a year in 1949–50 – an index for the relative wealth of the corresponding areas. Comparable data were not available for Canada.

The three main clusters of the US part of the Great Lakes megalopolis are quite prominent whereas the various small clusters, especially those towards the south and southwest, appear greatly reduced in importance. Similar observations can be made in terms of aggregate income distribution.

The emphasis given to manufacturing in the Great Lakes megalopolis was examined by using the percentage of employed population in manufacturing in 1960. This showed perhaps better than other variables the various parts of the megalopolis interconnected in the manner of the Eastern megalopolis. Farther to the northeast a cluster around Buffalo–Hamilton–Toronto is prominent. Several clusters to the south, including Cincinnati–Dayton, are also apparent. The Mohawk "bridge" is lightly indicated. Canadian clusters to the northeast also appear – notably Montreal and its eastern extensions. Here again the emphasis is on the three main clusters, namely Chicago, Detroit, and Cleveland–Pittsburgh, where manufacturing activity accounts for more than 30 per cent of employment.

The east coast megalopolis is completely evident, with emphasis upon Baltimore–New Jersey and New York.

Figure 5 shows the main road network, including Canada. In the Eastern megalopolis a lengthwise axis is well developed. In the Great Lakes megalopolis a central axis connects Chicago through Toledo with Cleveland and Pittsburgh. Detroit is joined to this main axis through a perpendicular connection. There is also a direct link between Chicago and Detroit.

The main road connections between the Eastern megalopolis and the Great Lakes megalopolis take place through two links: to the south, from Philadelphia to Pittsburgh, over the Appalachian Mountains; and to the north through the Mohawk Valley. Although offering a more direct connection, the southern link runs through unfavourable topography, whereas the roundabout Mohawk connection has easier grades.

COMPARATIVE ANALYSIS OF
URBANIZED AREAS IN THE GREAT LAKES AND
EAST COAST MEGALOPOLISES

Because of the importance of the urbanized area concept as defined by the US Bureau of the Census, a tabulation of the more characteristic data by urbanized areas is reproduced here. Table 1 shows 1960 data for the seven most populated urbanized areas of the Great Lakes and Eastern megalopolis regions.

The seven largest urbanized areas in the Canadian extension of the Great Lakes megalopolis are listed in Table 2. For Canada, the nearest equivalent – census metropolitan areas – was used. In this respect, relatively few statistics are comparable for the United States and Canada.

The relevant phenomena are reproduced in Fig. 6 and permit the following comparisons:

Land Area   7.3 per cent larger for the Eastern megalopolis; primarily because of the very large area of the New York–northeastern New Jersey urbanized area.

Total Population   The population of the urbanized areas

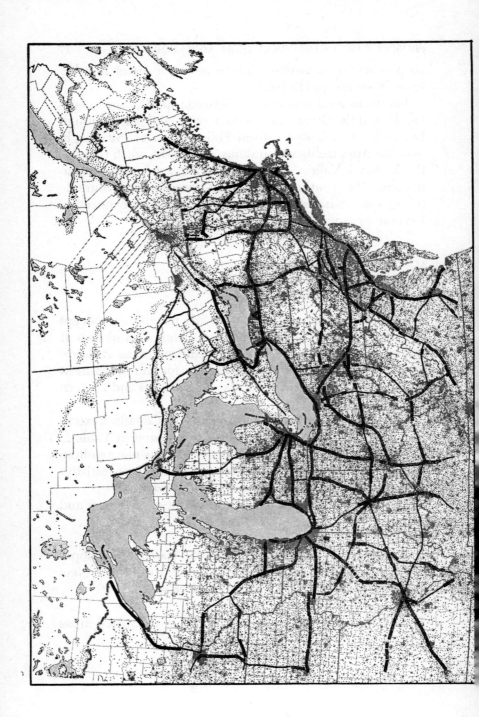

AS OF SEPTEMBER 30, 1964

— Completed Interstate
(4 Lane Canada)

— Major Toll Roads

— Under Construction Interstate
(4 Lane Canada)

— Proposed Interstate

------- Major Two Lane Highway of
Canada (As of 1961)

URBANIZED AREAS

🔹 Extent of areas

RURAL POPULATION

. 500 inh.

. 1,000-2,500

URBAN POPULATION
IN PLACES OUTSIDE
URBANIZED AREAS

. 25,000-50,000

. 10,000-25,000

⊙ 2,500-10,000

MILES
100 50 0   100   200   300   400   500   1000

FIG. 5   Major highway network, 1964.

TABLE 1

Comparison of Great Lakes and East Coast urbanized areas[1] by selected characteristics

Urbanized areas	Area	Population, 1960						1959 Income				Other selected socio-economic characteristics				Housing units 1960				Occupied housing units	
	Land area (sq. miles)	US rank	Total (1,000)	Per sq. mile	Increase, 1950-60 (%)	Non-white (%)	Median age years	Median income ($)	Under $3,000 (%)	$10,000 and over (%)	Aggregate income in 1959 of population, 1960 ($ million)	Median school years completed 25 years old and over, 1960	Unemployment of civilian labour force, 1960 (%)	Of total employment in mfg. (%), 1960	Of total mfg. employment in durable goods industries, 1960 (%)	In one-unit structures (%)	In structures built in 1950 or later (%)	With air conditioning (%)	With automobile (%)	Median value of owner-occupied units ($)	Median gross rent of renter-occupied units ($ monthly)
	1	2	3	4	5	6	7	8	9	10	11	12	13	14	15	16	17	18	19	20	21
Great Lakes																					
Chicago–Northwestern Indiana	959.8	3	5,959	6,209	21.1	16.1	31.3	7,292	10.7	25.7	14,572	10.8	4.4	35.2	63.7	43.1	22.1	14.7	70.4	18,600	89
Detroit	731.9	5	3,538	4,834	28.6	15.8	29.6	6,888	13.6	22.0	7,621	10.8	7.9	40.7	82.4	74.3	28.9	6.8	82.1	13,300	79
Pittsburgh	525.0	9	1,804	3,437	17.7	8.1	32.4	6,106	13.8	17.1	3,667	10.8	6.8	35.9	80.6	71.7	20.5	6.8	74.1	12,900	69
Cleveland	586.7	10	1,785	3,042	29.0	14.7	31.4	6,967	11.1	22.4	4,154	11.1	5.3	39.4	72.8	62.6	25.2	8.9	79.8	17,700	84
Milwaukee	392.0	14	1,150	2,934	38.6	5.8	30.1	7,036	9.4	21.0	2,636	11.2	3.9	40.8	73.1	54.7	28.4	7.8	77.9	16,500	89
Buffalo	160.2	16	1,054	6,582	17.7	8.1	30.3	6,394	12.6	16.8	2,148	10.4	6.9	38.4	64.0	49.3	20.6	5.1	76.3	14,800	74
Cincinnati	242.3	17	994	4,101	22.2	13.6	30.5	6,317	15.1	18.4	2,108	10.3	4.7	32.9	56.3	54.0	21.0	10.0	72.6	15,500	68
TOTAL (average)	3,597.9		16,284	4,526	24.0	13.6	30.9	6,889[2]	12.0	22.2	36,906	10.6	5.7	37.3	69.8	56.8	24.0	10.1	75.3	16,000	83
East Coast																					
New York–N.E. New Jersey	1,891.5	1	14,115	7,462	14.8	11.5	33.9	6,675	12.4	22.7	34,139	10.6	4.7	29.2	43.1	31.8	19.5	15.0	58.6	17,800	76
Philadelphia	896.7	4	3,635	4,092	24.4	17.5	32.0	6,437	13.2	19.2	7,632	10.4	5.5	35.0	49.1	79.5	21.8	18.9	68.7	10,700	69
Boston	515.8	7	2,413	4,679	17.5	3.5	32.3	6,622	11.3	20.6	5,365	12.1	3.8	28.8	52.9	43.9	14.0	5.8	71.7	15,800	82
Washington	340.7	8	1,808	5,308	40.5	25.9	29.4	7,003	10.3	30.7	4,615	12.3	2.9	7.6	36.7	56.5	35.6	25.7	73.5	17,100	88
Baltimore	220.3	12	1,419	6,441	22.1	24.4	30.1	6,319	14.3	17.2	2,805	9.5	4.1	31.5	63.0	75.9	26.0	12.5	69.0	10,500	77
Providence–Pawtucket, R.I.–Mass.	188.0	26	660	3,508	13.1	2.2	33.2	5,588	15.7	12.4	1,229	10.1	5.1	40.9	60.2	49.0	16.5	4.8	78.6	12,300	62
Norfolk–Portsmouth, Va.	108.6	36	508	4,676	31.9	26.5	24.7	5,075	27.1	11.1	835	10.6	5.1	16.2	64.6	72.2	35.6	14.1	73.5	11,000	72
TOTAL (average)	3,861.6		24,558	6,360	17.7	13.4	32.7	6,524[2]	12.6	21.7	56,620	10.5	4.6	26.5	50.7	45.1	21.0	14.9	65.1	15,200	76

Source: US Dept. of Commerce, Bureau of the Census, *County and City Data Book,* 1962.
[1] Only the seven largest USA urbanized areas of each included.
[2] Average family incomes ($): Great Lakes 8,887; East Coast 8,959. Per capita income ($): Great Lakes 2,266; East Coast 2,306.

TABLE 2

Comparison of Canadian metropolitan areas[1] by selected characteristics

Census metropolitan areas	Canadian rank	Population, 1961		Family income, 1961			Occupied dwellings, 1961		Manufacturing employment, 1961
		Total (1,000)	Increase 1951–61 (%)	Average income ($)	Under $3,000 (%)	$10,000 and over (%)	Single detached (%)	With automobile (%)	Labor force in manufacturing (%)
Montreal	1	2,110	43.3	6,046	17.2	10.9	19.5	54.1	32.4
Toronto	2	1,824	50.7	6,542	14.1	12.1	55.7	72.9	32.3
Ottawa	5	430	46.9	6,643	12.6	13.0	48.3	72.9	13.2
Hamilton	6	395	41.0	6,030	14.7	8.5	73.0	77.0	46.3
Quebec	7	358	29.4	5,801	19.2	10.2	29.2	55.2	20.7
Windsor	10	193	18.2	5,384	20.6	6.7	75.2	73.6	43.1
London	12	181	40.6	5,985	14.4	8.5	66.9	76.3	27.7
Total average		5,491	43.6	6,189	15.7	11.0	42.1	65.1	31.4

Source: Census of Canada, 1961.
[1] Based on areas defined for the 1961 Census; only the seven largest areas in the Great Lakes vicinity included.

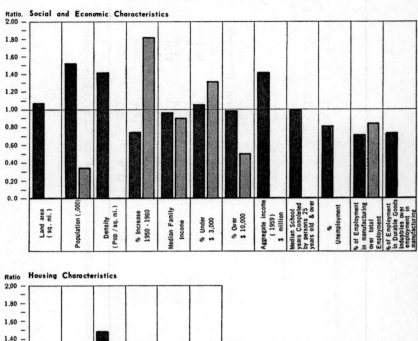

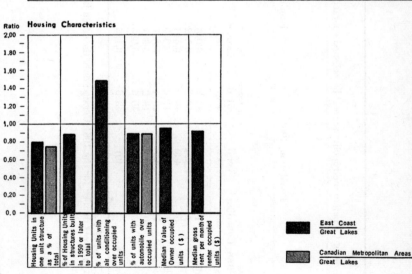

FIG. 6 Comparison of selected characteristics among major urban areas.

in the main clusters of the Eastern megalopolis is considerably greater; 24.9 million inhabitants compared to 16.3 million in the US part of the Great Lakes megalopolis. The latter has three times the population of its Canadian extension. The distribution of population among urbanized areas is much more uneven in the Eastern megalopolis, where New York surpasses the rest, with the second largest city, Philadelphia, one-third its size. Within the Great Lakes megalopolis, Detroit is only 40 per cent smaller than Chicago. Within the Canadian extension, Montreal is only 17 per cent larger than Toronto, but inequalities between these cities and the remaining census metropolitan areas are very great.

Population Density Densities are higher in the Eastern megalopolis, exceeding those of the Great Lakes by about 40 per cent (6,360 inhabitants per square mile as compared with 4,526). The various urbanized areas differ among themselves and this variation is considerably greater in the Great Lakes area. Buffalo, with the highest density in the Great Lakes megalopolis, ranks second to New York, which has the highest density of all.

Population Growth 1950–60 A much more rapid overall population increase is noticed in the Great Lakes megalopolis, 24.0 per cent vs. 17.7 per cent for the Eastern megalopolis. More uniform figures are found in the Great Lakes megalopolis, whereas the spread in the Eastern megalopolis is larger. The largest figure, 40.5 per cent, is found in Washington; the lowest, 8.0 per cent, in Boston – both in the Eastern megalopolis. In the Great Lakes megalopolis the highest percentage increase, that for Milwaukee, is only slightly lower than that for Washington; those for Cleveland and Detroit, the next highest, are higher than all the

Eastern rates of growth except those for Washington and Norfolk. Since Milwaukee can be regarded as a fringe area of the Chicago complex, this means that Cleveland and Detroit are the fastest growing urbanized areas of the Great Lakes megalopolis. It may be characteristic that the two urbanized areas with the lowest increase, Pittsburgh and Buffalo, show a percentage increase exactly equal to the average for the Eastern megalopolis. In other words, the lowest percentage increases in the Great Lakes megalopolis (Buffalo and Pittsburgh) are higher than those of New York, Providence, and Boston, or the entire northern section of the Eastern megalopolis.

Canadian increases surpass even those of the US components of the Great Lakes megalopolis. The highest (50.7 per cent) is in Toronto, a fact of particular importance for the future development of the Canadian extension.

Medium Family Income   This is approximately on the same level in both megalopolitan areas, being only slightly higher in the Great Lakes. Average family and per capita incomes, however, are higher on the east coast.

In the Canadian extension, average family incomes are lower but evenly distributed among census metropolitan areas.

Aggregate Income   Taking into consideration that family or per capita incomes are roughly on the same level, while population is considerably higher in the Eastern megalopolis, it follows that aggregate income is considerably higher there – by about 55 per cent. New York has almost as much aggregate income as all seven urbanized areas of the Great Lakes.

Median School Years   Median exposure to education is at approximately the same level in both areas. There are no important differences among the various urbanized areas, except that Baltimore is considerably lower and Boston and Washington considerably higher than the Eastern megalopolis average.

Employment Structure and Unemployment In 1960, unemployment in the Great Lakes area was more than 20 per cent higher, with the highest percentage in Detroit, followed by Buffalo and Pittsburgh. All exceed Baltimore, which has the highest rate for the Eastern megalopolis. This may be related to the considerably higher percentage of population employed in manufacturing, particularly in durable goods. Such activities are more vulnerable to recession and structural changes such as automation. However, the correlation is less apparent when individual urbanized areas are examined, because of special factors influencing each case.

Employment in manufacturing is considerably higher in the Great Lakes megalopolis (37.3 per cent) than in the Eastern megalopolis (26.5 per cent). Of these totals, 69.3 per cent is in durable goods in the Great Lakes and 50.7 per cent on the east coast. Detroit has the highest percentage of manufacturing employment in durable goods (82.4 per cent) whereas Washington has only 7.6 per cent of total employment in manufacturing. In the Canadian extension, Windsor and Hamilton have the highest percentage.

Housing Units In view of the population trend during recent decades, it is only natural that the percentage of new houses is higher in the Great Lakes than in the Eastern megalopolis. Differences between urbanized areas are not marked in the Great Lakes, where Detroit and Milwaukee head the list, but are pronounced on the east coast, where Boston has only 14 per cent of new houses compared with 35.6 for Washington. There is a close relationship between age of housing and rates of population increase.

The percentage of single-unit detached houses, an index of the suburban type of urban development, is considerably higher in the US Great Lakes megalopolis than in the Eastern (56.8 and 45.1 per cent, respectively), and even lower (42.1 per cent) in the Canadian extension. Nevertheless, the urbanized areas with the highest percentages of single-unit detached houses are found in the Eastern megalopolis (Philadelphia 79.5 per cent, Baltimore 75.9 per cent). Detroit ranks highest (74.3 per cent) in the Great Lakes. The Canadian census of metropolitan areas displays great divergencies, ranging from 19.5 per cent (Montreal) to 75.2 per cent (Windsor).

Change in Population Densities 1950–60 Densities within the two megalopolitan areas are falling, since urban land is increasing at a much higher rate than urban population. The decrease in population densities is considerably faster in the Eastern megalopolis, which has the highest overall density, so that an equalization process is apparently taking place.

Population growth during the past fifty years in the main clusters that form the Great Lakes and Eastern megalopolises is shown in Table 3.

The Great Lakes megalopolis has grown at a much more rapid pace (2.15 per cent) than the Eastern megalopolis for which the average yearly growth rate is 1.52 per cent: in other words, the population of the Great Lakes megalopolis has trebled in half a century while that of the east coast megalopolis has slightly more than doubled.

In fact, the Great Lakes megalopolis has grown faster than the Eastern in every decade except 1930–40, the depression years. For its three main clusters, the highest increase during the last two decades occurred around Detroit. In the Eastern megalopolis the highest increase was recorded in the Washington–Philadelphia cluster in 1940–50 and the New York cluster in 1950–60.

The time lag between comparable phenomena for the two areas has been considerably greater in the past. Initially it must have been greater than fifty years, then it progressively decreased to its present lag of about thirty years for most variables. In general, the Great Lakes megalopolis constitutes a younger but more rapidly growing version of the Eastern megalopolis.

The younger age of the Great Lakes megalopolis can be seen in the comparatively long distance separating its three main clusters. The more advanced Eastern megalopolis consists of much closer clusters, so that the distances between them either disappear for certain variables or are quite small for others. As the Great Lakes megalopolis grows its clusters will spread outward from the nuclei and their links will join in the manner of the Eastern megalopolis.

This decrease of the time lag in the future is also anticipated by other studies, including the projections for the main regions of the USA made by the US Bureau of the Census and other sources. According to these projections, the population of the Great Lakes area is expected to catch up with the mid-Atlantic region (covering the east coast megalopolis) by the end of this century.

CONCLUSIONS

This brief study of the Great Lakes megalopolis has shown the importance of developments in this area and its extensions. Its rapid growth will enable it to compete soon for first place among the most important areas in the USA and

TABLE 3

Comparison of population growth between the us Great Lakes and Eastern megalopolises, 1910–1960 (thousands of persons)

	1910	1920	1930	1940	1950	1960
Chicago area	3,463	4,494	6,053	6,293	7,254	8,903
Detroit area	1,304	2,263	3,674	3,973	4,983	6,232
Cleveland–Pittsburgh area	2,737	3,710	5,073	5,211	5,722	6,558
Great Lakes	7,504	10,467	14,800	15,477	17,959	21,693
Boston area	3,106	3,561	4,047	4,316	4,679	5,064
New York area	7,701	9,375	11,947	12,991	14,488	16,725
Washington–Philadelphia area	4,378	5,266	6,528	7,132	8,594	10,493
East coast	15,185	18,202	22,522	24,439	27,761	32,282

Source: us Department of Commerce, Bureau of the Census.

Canada and to become a focal point of many economic and other activities on the North American continent.

A comparison of the various phenomena in the figures shows the formation of certain clusters within the Great Lakes megalopolis, with three major clusters centred around Chicago, Detroit, and Cleveland–Pittsburgh. These clusters are considered to form the main portion of the Great Lakes megalopolis.

A Canadian extension north of the Great Lakes, via London towards the Toronto, Montreal–Ottawa, and Quebec clusters, is also evident and qualifies the international character of this megalopolis.

A number of clusters to the south, southwest, and west of the Great Lakes megalopolis, such as the Cincinnati–Dayton–Columbus cluster, appear consistently and prominently. Although this latter cluster is related to the Great Lakes megalopolis, and is growing much faster than the three clusters within the main us portion of it, it is not possible to predict whether it will become directly connected with it and if so what kind of connection this will be.

The Mohawk "bridge" stands out on a number of maps. In view of the expected rapid development of both the Eastern and the Great Lakes megalopolises, at least one bridge connecting these two areas is likely to develop: a connection south of Lake Erie from Cleveland to Buffalo, Albany, Massachusetts, and Connecticut. This link will probably be strengthened by the increasing importance of the Canadian extension of the Great Lakes megalopolis, especially in the rapidly growing Toronto–Hamilton–Buffalo cluster. The Buffalo–Albany arc, therefore, will offer two different connections westward, one towards Toronto into Canada north of the lakes and another one south of the lakes towards Cleveland and the main portion of the megalopolis.

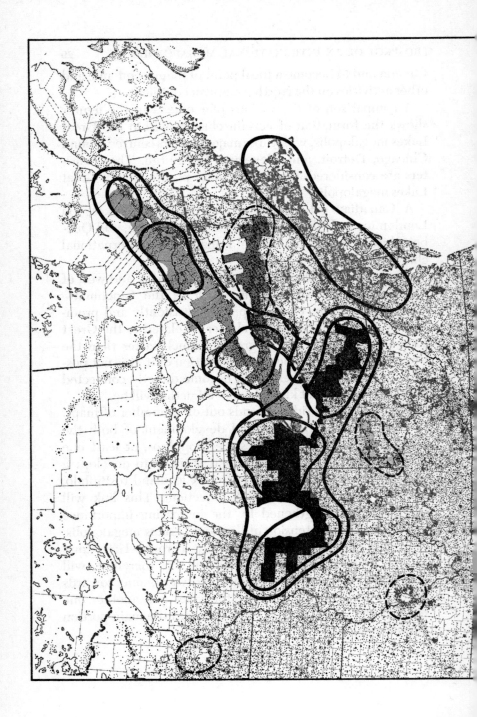

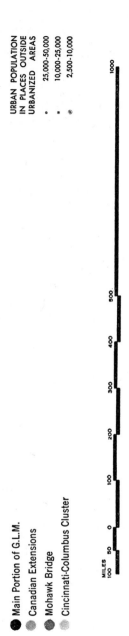

RURAL POPULATION
·   500 inh.
▪   1,000-2,500

URBAN POPULATION
IN PLACES OUTSIDE
URBANIZED AREAS
●   25,000-50,000
▪   10,000-25,000
◉   2,500-10,000

● Main Portion of G.L.M.
  Canadian Extensions
  Mohawk Bridge
  Cincinnati-Columbus Cluster

MILES
100 50   0   100   200   300   400   500   1000

FIG. 7   Tentative boundaries of the Great Lakes megalopolis and its probable extensions.

The exact delimitations of the areas to be included in the Great Lakes megalopolis and its extensions cannot be determined at this point. Many more detailed studies will be needed before such a precise delimitation can be reached. A provisional delimitation, however, is shown in Fig. 7.

Comments on the Doxiadis Report

MAURICE F. PARKINS

MY UNDERSTANDING of the megalopolitan problem stems from the cumulative effect of my own experience as a student of urban affairs, both of the United States and of other countries as an urban planner with public agencies and as a private practitioner; and from other insights, spread over a time long enough for gaining an historical perspective.

Actually, we know very little about the phenomenon of the international megalopolis and its dynamics. The word "megalopolis" was first used by an ancient philosopher of Alexandria, Philo Judaeus, who taught that there is a great "city of ideas" that predetermine and command the material world in which we live, and this great city of ideas Philo called "megalopolis." Lewis Mumford, our contemporary urban planning philosopher, in his *Culture of Cities* published in 1938, referred to "megalopolis" as the declining stage of "metropolis." He calls it "Alexandrianism," referring to the city of Alexandria which witnessed its decline in the third century BC. He also called it less complimentary names, such as a "defacement of the natural environment," a "paper dream city," a "sick metropolis." We see it next as the name given to the urbanized northeastern seaboard of the United States in a 1961 study by a French geographer, Jean Gottmann, entitled *Megalopolis*. Other writers have discussed this form of urbanization, but none as thoroughly as Dr. Gottmann. To me it is a type of multi-regional, multi-state, super urban-suburban agglomeration. An extremely complex phenomenon! a monster city that, if allowed to grow and develop without control, may eventually lead to self-extinction.

We are all aware of the intensity of the urbanization process as perhaps the most striking feature of industrial civilization, the relentless pressures of the population explosion, the growth and spread of the metropolitan areas, with the boundaries of the various municipalities – although they have separate administrations – diffusing and becoming one great urbanized continuum. But coupled with these pressures and demands is a pervading sense of purpose, an involvement in problems linking us to the affairs and needs and conditions of the human environment, of civilization, which is synonymous with the urban way of life, and with the world today.

I see megalopolis as the beginning of a new form of urban development, a trend, a new concept. I see it as a constant interplay of challenge and response, and as a motivating force of leadership in the modern world of science, of commerce, of technology, of art, of engineering, and the humanities. I see it also creeping up and down the Pacific Coast, as it does on the northeastern seaboard, between the Great Lakes and the Ohio River, in other regions of the USA, in Western Europe, and in other parts of the world. While I agree with Dr. Gottmann that the "new order to be developed could only be an urban order," it does not necessarily have to be all "commercial development, industrialization, mechanization, motorization and automation, on a large scale."

I can readily sympathize with Lewis Mumford's feelings when he posed the question, "Will urban life come to mean the further concentration of power in a few metropolises where ramifying suburban dormitories will finally swallow the rural hinterland?" I join the gentle philosopher in lamenting the fact, as he first did some thirty years ago, that "vast plans are afoot to continue this process."

A realistic and comprehensive understanding of the

international megalopolis rests, in the first instance, upon a recognition of its meaning in the United States. As a national concept, it should be understood in terms of its impact upon government, business, and industry, its economic dimensions, its impact on the planning of its main components, such as transportation and recreation. Internationally, the concept is then seen as a contribution to the continuing viability and strength of the participating nations as an extension of, and a stimulus to, trade and other co-operative efforts.

But the most important questions to ask here are, "Would this concept improve the economic welfare of the people? Would it provide for an optimum human resource development? Would it strengthen or weaken the metropolitan, regional, or national economy? Finally, if this urban form should be allowed to grow continuously and merge into one physical entity, would it be desirable?" Let us briefly examine several of these questions.

Dr. Gottmann has identified the emergence of a basically new form of human settlement, which he calls "megalopolis," that is the area of cities, towns, villages, and suburbs lying between southern New Hampshire and northern Virginia and from the Atlantic shore to the Appalachian foothills. It is often considered by urban students as a new "conurbation" – a metropolitan region formed by the coalescence of expanding neighbouring metropolitan areas.

Actually, this vast agglomeration to which Dr. Gottmann refers consists of a number of metropolitan areas separated by large tracts of farmland and woodland. Each of these metropolises is strongly oriented to and, at the same time, derives its identity from a single centre city. Because of the absence of these two characteristics – lack of interconnectedness and lack of centrality – some regional specialists think that the northeastern seaboard megalopolis is not a true conurbation, and that with the exception perhaps of Baltimore and Washington this condition is not likely to happen anywhere in North America in the twentieth century.* They regard chances for the Great Lakes urbanized areas to become a megalopolis or conurbation by the year 2000 as even more remote.

However, the available evidence does not support such a view; and I can see the whole of the northeastern seaboard as well as the Great Lakes area becoming big polynucleated cities, with the population continually expanding and rising in density. But such cities cannot exist without a strong "megalopolitan government" to control and administer them.

Megalopolis has baffled the serious students of it. Even Dr. Gottmann admits that "the concept of Megalopolis as an integrated system is difficult to realize, for there is so much rivalry between the various components within the region: states, cities, counties, entities, even townships."† Politically, it does not exist, yet it consists of thousands of political units. Geographically, it has no boundary. It has no common system of economic and social institutions. James Russell Wiggins speaks of it, "like the earth at its beginnings, without form or void. . . ."‡

Research on the process of agglomeration is needed to understand the historical process of megalopolis, and perhaps to suggest a basis for changing the process through effective metropolitan and regional planning. Answers are also needed to such questions as, "What is the structure and quality of life in it? What kind of activities go on there? What is its transportation system, its economic base, the

*Hans Blumenfeld, "The modern metropolis," *Scientific American*, September 1965, p. 72.

†Jean Gottmann, *Megalopolis*, 1961.

‡James Russell Wiggins, *Megalopolis, Man and Metro* (Washington, 1965).

needs of the people and the ways in which they are met?" From the physical planning point of view, I think such a vast, unbroken urban form of coalescent and overlapping metropolitan regions would be undesirable. It is the aim and objective of planning to ensure that urban dwellers live within reasonable distance of the open countryside and that there be reasonable access to recreational land. These social objectives are reinforced by economic objectives.

Research may also indicate how much the agglomeration process can be interfered with, and what will be the cost of so doing. One of the crucial questions is that of the administrative organization of planning. Finally, what are the alternatives to megalopolis? There is a need in the United States, as in most other countries, for metropolitan and regional planning.

Let me emphasize that no single solution, or single prescription, or single urban form will provide the whole answer in the rational accommodation of urban growth and change. I believe that the solution to many of the complexities of urbanization can be found in metropolitan and regional planning. Effective comprehensive planning of the metropolis and the regional areas calls for equally effective metropolitan or regional authorities. We have made only a modest beginning in co-ordinating metropolitan approaches to some specific problems, namely in Nashville, Tennessee, and Miami–Dade County, Florida. These examples are not as comprehensive as the Greater London Council, which was created in 1965 in England to co-ordinate planning and a wide variety of public programs throughout thirty-two boroughs, or the New York Area Regional Council, which was formed in late 1966. One of the goals of the "Great Society" is to find the means for orderly development and a livable environment in metropolitan areas. Area planning is a recognized means to this end.

As you are aware, the nation's population growth and spread across the urban landscape constitute both an immense challenge and an opportunity. The dynamics of this urbanization is causing concern to our government, affecting public policy and the very structure of society itself. By the year 2000 we will have rebuilt a major portion of the cities that now exist, and we will need to build as many new cities to satisfy our growing population.

To meet this challenge, we need a national policy on urban development; we need national planning goals and national objectives in key areas of our socio-economic structure, such as employment, housing, recreation, metropolitan growth. And finally we need the establishment of a federal agency or urban research institute, with the capabilities and resources of a NASA, or skilled technology companies to explore new approaches, devise new urban systems, develop mathematical models for analysis, prediction, and testing of public policies, and design and build new cities from scratch.

The planner of the future will find himself in a new role with respect to city-building. He will be the co-ordinator of systems designed to tie a total urban complex together. He will have to relate his skills to the development of these large-scale systems. His new clients may be systems-oriented companies like GE, who are designing and producing new cities, or local agencies or authorities, or the Committee for National Land Development Policy, which in July 1966 proposed construction of twenty-five new "molecular cities" of one million people each in the next thirty years. The planner's future may be with organizations such as these, where the real design decisions will be made in the next decade. The place of the planner may be with the bigger organization, to co-ordinate and integrate the various hardware and software systems that will make up the future urban complex.

As President Johnson has so well stated, "The prize – cities of spacious beauty and lively promise, where men are truly free to determine how they will live – is too rich to be lost, because the problems are complex. Let there be debate over the means and priorities. Let there be experiment with a dozen approaches, or a hundred. But let there be commitment to that goal."

Aristotle said: "Men come together in cities in order to live. They remain together in order to live the good life." Buckminster Fuller, the unorthodox genius of the climate-controlled bubble, extends this philosophy down to the present in the form of a challenge in his statement: "The greatest fact of the 20th Century is that we can make life on earth a good success for all men." Since life on earth will be lived mostly in the cities, this life could be ruthless, sterile, chaotic, full of despair and ugliness, or it could be the good life.

The choice is ours.

2. SHAPING THE GREAT LAKES–
ST. LAWRENCE HEARTLAND

Water and Power

HERB GRAY

THE CONCEPT OF an international megalopolis in the Great Lakes heartland provides us with one of the most exciting challenges of modern times. It could lead to the development of a true "great city" (as "megalopolis" is literally translated), whose existence would make it possible for millions of people to live richer and happier lives; or it could lead to these same millions being confined within a mammoth international urban sprawl, with all that this could mean in terms of ugliness, decay, and administrative chaos.

Which of these two directions will be taken by the Great Lakes heartland in its future development? Much of the answer will depend on decisions made and planning carried out now. Therefore, discussions at gatherings such as this seminar are valuable and important, as is the continuing work under various private auspices at universities and elsewhere. However, it is clear that the multiplicity of interests and administrative divisions within the area of any developing megalopolis would mean that action taken by governments, both now and in the future, will also be of particular importance.

The concept we are dealing with is, therefore, of great interest to me as an elected representative of an area that would be a key part of any Great Lakes megalopolis. In this capacity, I must have a primary concern for the people whose lives will be affected for better or for worse by the manner in which this new concept of urban life develops. Perhaps none of the factors linked with it will touch the lives of everyone within its boundaries more directly than those of power and water.

I hope to outline in general terms some of the problems connected with the areas of water and power, along with some of the work being done to solve them, and also to point to some of the steps planned for the future. My comments will indicate a Canadian point of view and, of course, will be those of a non-specialist.

Let me deal first with the question of power. This problem would have had much greater significance for a developing Great Lakes megalopolis ten years ago than it has today. At that time it appeared that the potential for further hydro-electric power development in the Great Lakes area was rapidly coming to an end. However, because of recent changes in technology, long-range transmission of hydro-electric power is becoming possible at reasonable cost. High-voltage transmission lines are able to span large slices of the continent and sites in areas such as Labrador and other remote locations can be looked to as sources of electricity for the Great Lakes region. These long-range transmission lines will undoubtedly form part of national power grids in each of our countries, upon which the megalopolis will draw to meet its growing needs for electric power. There will probably also be increasing exchanges of such power between different areas of this megalopolis to meet different patterns of demand.

This would mean, in any event, problems of co-ordination, especially insofar as these exchanges are across the international boundary. But any export of power from Canada would mean ensuring that our export is surplus to our own long-range requirements, with built-in guarantees where necessary for repatriation, and that such exports are paid for at prices reflecting the real value of this power in the market-place.

The development in a practical way of alternatives to hydro-electric power for various uses has helped to eliminate the threat of power shortages for the Great Lakes area.

There are immense reserves of oil and natural gas in western Canada, with major pipelines to move them to market. Natural gas provides an alternative form of energy for those industries requiring its particular properties, thereby reducing the demand for other sources of power. However, at the present time, it has not yet been developed to the stage where it is fully practical for conventional power plants.

Energy produced by atomic reactors provides a wider potential source of power than anything I have mentioned. The cost of atomic power is becoming more and more competitive and in the relatively near future this cost is expected to drop even further.

When we consider the size and population of the country and the high cost of nuclear research, the fact that Canada has been able to establish a position in the vanguard of the commercial use of atomic power can be considered a great national accomplishment. This achievement owes much to the action of our federal government. Federal funds have helped to build a nuclear power demonstration plant at Rolphton, Ontario, which has been operating since late 1962. Atomic Energy of Canada Limited, an agency of the federal government, is building this country's first full-scale nuclear-power station on the shore of Lake Huron, and is starting another in Quebec.

When we add our tremendous reserves of uranium to the sources of power already mentioned, it would appear that the Great Lakes area has no need to fear a shortage in meeting the demands of its growing population and industry.

However, the problem of its water supply cannot be disposed of with the same relative ease.

Until recently the general public took the resource of water for granted, assuming that there would never be any serious problem about its quantity and purity. It has come as a shock to many to realize that there are now areas on the North American Continent, including some in Canada, that are facing shortages of water. What to do about maintaining this vital resource has, therefore, become an important popular issue on both sides of the international border.

It can not be said that Canada as a whole is actually short of water, possessing as it does some twenty-five per cent of the world's supply of fresh water. If there is a problem, it is mainly one of meeting the need for clean water in populated areas.

From time immemorial man has used his rivers and streams both as a source of water and as a means of waste disposal. So long as populations were small and limited amounts of waste were discharged into these rivers and streams, no serious difficulties arose. The processes of nature were adequate to purify the effluents. But with the growth of cities and industries and the introduction of new kinds of pollutants, the system of natural purification broke down.

Most people tend to be concerned primarily with the obvious forms of water pollution – sewage, debris from industry, trash heedlessly thrown into streams. The emphasis, therefore, has been on construction of sewage disposal plants and on elimination of more conventional forms of industrial or other pollution. These steps are important, but the danger to our water supply created by new breeds of pollutants – detergents, waste created by new technologies, and the wash-off of fertilizers and pesticides – is just beginning to be recognized.

These creations of the mid-twentieth century have introduced a new factor because they not only pollute our waters, they also enrich them. In exactly the same way that a fertilizer enriches soil, it seems to render more fertile the water it enters. This results in an explosive growth of algae and aquatic plants. In this growth process, and even more in the process of decomposition, the vegetation serves to absorb the dissolved oxygen content of the water, without which desirable marine life cannot survive. Furthermore, since dissolved oxygen is an essential element in the natural cycle of water purification, its absorption slows that process. The result is a form of slow strangulation which causes the death of lakes and rivers.

There are, therefore, at least two elements to be considered in dealing with the problem of eliminating pollution. The first is to do away with what might be called the conventional or classic pollutants – sewage, industrial or other waste. The second is to keep pace with the new breed of pollutants created by our ever changing modern technology. These efforts involve individuals, industry, and all levels of government.

Time does not permit detailed discussion of how jurisdiction over water is divided among the various levels of government in Canada. However, this subject must be touched on, at least briefly, because the question of water cannot be isolated from its legal and constitutional implications.

Under Canadian constitutional practice, natural resources, including water, have been thought to come within the jurisdiction of the provinces. Therefore, the provinces, which are responsible for municipal affairs as well, must deal with the problem of water pollution, exclusive, of course, of that in international waters. The federal government has direct jurisdiction over boundary or international waters as well as responsibilities involving water which

stem from its constitutional jurisdiction over fisheries, transportation, navigation, international and interprovincial
trade, and criminal law. It can be seen that there is bound
to be some overlapping of jurisdiction and that co-operation
and consultation among all three levels of government are
essential.

Each of the provinces has laws dealing with pollution, as
do most municipalities. While there may be a need for additional legislation, the problem in many cases is not so much
an absence of law as it is a lack of either appropriate regulations under the existing law, or of its effective enforcement.

The Ontario Water Resources Commission is considered
one of the more effective bodies of its type in North
America. Its activities, together with certain federal government programs, to which I will refer in a moment, have
helped many Ontario municipalities to have modern secondary sewage treatment facilities. It is expected that all
municipalities in the Great Lakes region will have such
installations in the not too distant future. Furthermore,
under existing laws, which are now being enforced more
actively, no new industry which might pollute waters is
permitted to establish itself in Ontario without adequate
depollution facilities. Laws requiring water purification in
existing plants are also being more and more widely enforced. The federal government provides tax incentives to
encourage industry to construct anti-pollution facilities. It
can be said, therefore, that progress is being made in dealing with the problem of industrial water pollution in the
Canadian section of the Great Lakes area.

I should like to review briefly a number of federal government programs aimed at fighting industrial and municipal
water pollution.

To assist municipalities to finance the construction of
sewage treatment plants, Central Mortgage and Housing
Corporation, the federal housing agency, makes loans for

periods of up to fifty years at low rates of interest in an amount up to 65 per cent of the cost of such plants. Twenty-five per cent of these loans is forgiven if construction is completed by a given date. During the five years that this program has been in operation, approximately 1,000 loans have been granted, totalling over $200 million. More than half of these loans in number and dollar value have been made in Ontario.

Through its winter works program, the federal government advances funds to municipalities for various projects, including the construction of sewage treatment systems. Some $65 million have been contributed in this manner since 1958. It has also created a tax incentive to encourage industry to construct or install anti-pollution equipment. Industry is allowed to write off such equipment at the accelerated rate of 50 per cent per annum.

Under various federal laws, including the Fisheries Acts, the Canada Shipping Act, the Criminal Code, the Oil Pollution Prevention Regulations of the Navigable Waters Protection Act, the government prohibits activities which cause pollution of waters, and has been intensifying its enforcement activities, particularly with regard to oil pollution from ships. Through the International Joint Commission, it co-operates closely with both the United States and provincial authorities in the control of pollution affecting international waters, particularly in the Great Lakes.

Research on the causes and effects of pollution and on methods of dealing with them is carried on constantly and is expanding rapidly. While much important work in the field of research has already been undertaken, much still needs to be done to determine the nature of pollution and the most effective way of dealing with its various forms. As I have mentioned, one reason for this is the new breed of pollutants created by changing technology.

There are similar problems all across the country. It is

logical, therefore, that our federal government is giving special attention to basic research on the effects of pollution, its treatment, and design of equipment to deal with it. The results of this work are made available to the provinces, which can then create their own programs without wasteful duplication of effort.

It is interesting to note that over $1½ million was invested in the study of the lower Great Lakes in 1966, with 90 per cent of the cost being borne by the federal government. This investment is expected to reach $5 million by 1970.

The Canadian Council of Resource Ministers is a relatively new agency of federal-provincial co-operation. Its organization and methods might provide a useful example of the techniques to be used by the various jurisdictions that will co-ordinate the activities of any future Great Lakes megalopolis. The IJC is another. The Council represents a trend towards the kind of co-operative federalism in Canada which, in view of the multiplicity of jurisdictions, is essential for the proper management of water and other renewable resources. It is an advisory and consultative body whose purpose is to achieve co-ordination of policies and programs in the field of renewable resources. Its membership is made up of representatives of the federal and provincial governments, and it is supported by its own secretariat.

A major conference on pollution was organized by the Council and took place in Montreal in 1966. It is hoped that this conference will lead to a more effective and co-ordinated national program for dealing with pollution.

Since it took many decades to create the present degree of water pollution, the problem cannot be solved overnight. To deal with it will eventually cost many millions of dollars. The magnitude of the problem and its urgency, however, are now realized at every level in both of our countries and effective steps are being taken. However, I do not feel that every possible avenue of research must be explored to the end before further action programs are put into effect in Canada, by both federal and provincial governments. There is room at the present time for additional positive steps. Continuing and increasing efforts are necessary to ensure that there will be an adequate supply of clean water to meet the needs of the population of any Great Lakes megalopolis.

There are those, however, who ask whether the existing supply of water, even if pollution is removed, will be sufficient for the requirements of the expanding population of North America, particularly its burgeoning urban areas such as that projected for the Great Lakes heartland. The experts do not appear to have a definite answer for us.

Of course the first step is to stop wasting the water presently available. This means not only keeping our waters clean; it also means conserving our natural supplies. Major sums are, in fact, being disbursed on flood control and water conservation projects by all three levels of government. Under the Canada Water Conservation Assistance Act the Canadian government contributes 37½ per cent of the cost of approved major projects in this field. The provincial government contributes an equal sum, with the local authority generally paying the remaining 25 per cent. Projects under this plan are now in progress in the Great Lakes area.

But there are those who continue to ask the question, "What if there is still a shortage?" in spite of measures such as those outlined above.

Approximately 60 per cent of Canada's fresh water flow occurs in its sparsely populated northern regions. Since these waters flow north, they are at present of no benefit to most of our population. There has therefore been a suggestion, particularly in the United States, that these northern waters be diverted southward. Those making the suggestion undoubtedly have in mind water shortages in the southwestern United States and in other parts of that country. They have also claimed that this measure might be useful in stabilizing the level of the Great Lakes. This concept of water diversion from northern Canada is evoking a great deal of public interest, which has been sparked by the publicity given to the so called NAWAPA (North American Water and Power Alliance) concept. This is estimated to involve a cost of $100 billion. There have been other diversion schemes mentioned as well. It should be stressed that neither the NAWAPA scheme nor any of the others have been put forward with the support of either the United States or Canadian governments.

How practical are these schemes? To what extent could they or alternatives be used to supplement the water supply in the Great Lakes region or in other parts of the continent?

It seems to me that before these questions can even be considered, there are two other more important questions that must be answered: "How much water do we actually have in Canada, and how much of it will be required to meet the needs of every section of our own country over the entire range of the foreseeable future?" These are questions of crucial importance—for example, could one have guessed, even a few years ago, the magnitude of the water requirements in Saskatchewan to develop its potash industry. Therefore, if we are to consider the question of diversion at all, we must first have answers to these two basic questions.

The federal government, in co-operation with the government of Ontario, is now engaged on a study of Ontario's northern rivers. These investigations are expected to show how much water is available and what the needs for the region will be. It is hoped that similar studies will soon be begun on the rivers of northern Quebec and other parts of Canada.

Obviously, time will be required to complete this water inventory and forecast of requirements. Only then can we begin to judge what surplus, if any, exists, and it is only then that investigation might possibly be warranted into the feasibility of one or other of the diversion schemes mentioned. In my view, any immediate study of diversion of Canada's northern waters would be premature in spite of calls for such investigations, particularly from the United States. If there is any diversion southward of Canadian waters in the future, it will certainly not be in the near future. We must first be sure that we have enough water in Canada to fill every Canadian need for every contingency of the foreseeable future. Discussion of diversions must be based on benefits to Canada equal in value in the marketplace after all possible Canadian requirements are met.

I should mention another possible way of augmenting our water supply, and that is re-use or re-cycling. This concept comes from the recognition that different types of water use require different standards of quality and purity. For example, the purity of the water for drinking must meet higher standards than that of water for swimming; similarly, water for irrigation need not meet the standards for swimming. By re-cycling water for secondary usage, in which equivalent purity or cleanliness is not essential, a greater amount becomes available to meet existing and expanding needs. This represents a relatively new approach to the problem of water shortages. However, to be effective, standards must be established indicating the minimal requirements of cleanliness for each specific use.

The recently created federal Department of Energy, Mines and Resources will undoubtedly have a key role to play in dealing with many of the problems of a developing Great Lakes megalopolis. The administration of water resources is obviously a matter of great complexity. No less than ten federal departments, together with a number of agencies dealing with this matter in one way or another, have grown up over the years. The government, therefore, in its departmental re-organization, placed responsibility for integrating and co-ordinating all federal activities in the field of water with this new key department (which also assumed similar responsibility in the fields of energy and of resources generally). This department succeeds the former Department of Mines and Technical Surveys which had been concerned with water and its problems. Three branches of the new department will occupy themselves with the field of water:

A The Marine Sciences branch, which is itself divided into three sections: the Hydrographic service which produces nautical charts; the Oceanographic division which studies Canadian coastal waters and the adjacent oceans; and the Ships division which operates the vessels to activate the work of the first two divisions.

B The Water Research branch, which was established in September 1965, and is still in the process of organization. Its Ground Water section carries on studies of occurrences, source, movement, and composition of ground water. Its Industrial Waters section carries out water quality studies with emphasis on pollution and develops procedures for water treatment in industrial usage. Its Glaciology section concentrates on monitoring glacier melt-off and accumulation. Other sections are now in the process of being manned and developed.

C The Water Resources branch, which was taken over from the former Department of Northern Affairs and National Resources. Its functions are many, including studies of stream flow and water levels. It conducts hydraulic and hydrologic studies for efficient water use, provides advice on water to other federal departments, administers federal water power, water conservation, and international water legislation, and maintains and develops water power resources inventory. The administration of the Canada Water Conservation Assistance Act also comes within its jurisdiction.

In addition to the work carried out specifically by these branches, the new department integrates and co-ordinates all federal responsibility in the area of water and water pollution, including the work of other departments such as National Health and Welfare, and Transport. It strives for the greatest possible co-operation between the federal government and the provinces and enables the entire field of water and its problems to be tackled with more efficiency and vigour at the federal level.

To meet the requirements of an emerging megalopolis for water and power will not be a simple task, but it should be a task more challenging than frightening. To carry it out successfully there must be further research programs. However, even while this research is being carried out, action that makes use of the knowledge we already have can and must be taken. Above all, there must be intensive planning now and in the future.

A Great Lakes megalopolis will spread across existing local, provincial, state, and even national boundaries. This entails a high degree of co-operation, co-ordination, and decision-making by governments, using techniques which may not yet be fully evolved or which may not even now exist. In working out these techniques, it is necessary to take into account the realities of the existence of our two national sovereignties. On the Canadian side of the border, the federal government may well have to play a larger role in co-ordination and planning, if not in outright action and administration in the area of urban affairs, than it does at present. This might require constitutional change – a complex question in Canada at any time – or at the very least more creative use of the constitutional jurisdiction it presently has in fields such as navigation and boundary waters.

While we have been talking about the resources of water and power, the primary concern of the modern democratic state must, of course, be for its people. This kind of concern is ultimately what the city as a positive and creative concept is all about. As Shakespeare said in *Coriolanus*, "the people are the city."

The growing role of governments in dealing with the problems of megalopolis is probably inevitable, but this should not necessarily be a cause for worry, if the people participate actively in the governments of their cities.

Dr. Doxiadis comes to us from Athens. A key part of his inspiration undoubtedly has been provided by the living memory of its golden age which surrounds his life and work in his native city of Athens. The citizens in this golden age, I am told, would pledge themselves to the service of their city by swearing an oath which said in part: "We shall strive unceasingly to quicken the public sense of civic duty; that in all these ways, we may pass on this city, greater, better, more beautiful than it came to us."

We would do well to remember these words when working to meet the challenge of an emerging international megalopolis in the Great Lakes heartland.

Water Pollution in the Detroit–Windsor Area in the Year 2000

JAMES P. HARTT

THIS PAPER IS AN ANSWER to those people who do not believe that water pollution is a serious problem and to those who believe that it could be corrected overnight if we were only willing to spend the necessary money. For the purpose of this study, I have chosen an area that coincides as nearly as possible with the urban Detroit area, which is referred to as the UDA in the Doxiadis report. Since I am most interested in the pollution situation in the Detroit–Windsor regional area, I must omit parts of the UDA which drain away from this area and thus do not contribute directly to the pollution in this region, and likewise include some areas outside the UDA which do contribute. This is why I have included a small part of Indiana and the northwest part of Ohio, both of which lie within the Maumee drainage basin; and also the Sydenham and Thames drainage basins in Ontario, even though they lie partly outside the UDA. Nonetheless they are contributors to the pollution in the Detroit–Windsor regional area, which includes the waterways of the St. Clair River, Lake St. Clair, the Detroit River, and the western tip of Lake Erie. Now that we have defined the area, let us look at some of the indicators of what the future has in store for us.

POPULATION TRENDS FROM 1960 TO 2000

Since 1960 was the last census year in the USA, and 1961 in Ontario, I have projected from these years to the year 2000. This has been done by taking into account state and provincial population forecasts and others that included 1980 and in some cases 1985, by independent agencies, and extrapolating beyond these years to 2000 (Table 1). In brief the situation is as follows:

The population in this drainage area, including parts of Michigan, Ohio, Indiana, and Ontario, was approximately 6,350,000 in 1960–61. In the year 2000, if expected rates of growth prevail, the population will be 12,150,000. Thus it will almost double in a period of forty years with over 80 per cent of the growth occurring in the urban areas of the region. Since we have not felt the full impact of the Seaway as yet, these figures may be low.

TABLE 1

Population predictions for the drainage basins tributary to the Detroit–Windsor regional area

State or Province	Populations for the indicated years		
	1960–1961	1980–1986	2000
Indiana	283,800 (60)	404,900 (85)	506,900
Michigan	4,502,100 (60)	6,196,700 (85)	8,287,700
Ohio	876,500 (60)	1,190,400 (80)	1,624,700
Ontario	703,000 (61)	1,238,000 (86)	1,726,000
TOTALS	6,365,400		12,145,300

Note: The population figures for all but the year 2000 are from data received from appropriate governmental agencies. The values for the year 2000 are extrapolated from the aforementioned data.

WASTE-WATER QUANTITIES EXPECTED

Does this population growth mean that we are apt to double the quantity of waste water produced in the same forty-year span? I am afraid it means much more than that. Using figures of the US Department of Commerce, Business and Defense Services Administration, we find that, while the population is expected to increase by just over 29 per cent from 1960 to 1980, the water usage in the same period is expected to increase by 53 per cent. This would indicate that water usage is increasing at a rate almost double the rate of population growth. This trend is to be expected, since water usage has been increasing more rapidly than population for more than sixty years. Although water usage is difficult to predict, since the rate of increase during the decades from 1900 has shown wide fluctuations while population growth has been more uniform, the overwhelming evidence points to a much more rapid increase in water use (and waste-water production) than in population between now and the year 2000. This would mean that water usage will likely increase about 1.83 times as fast as the population. Thus in the year 2000, when the population has increased to 192 per cent of what it was in 1960, water usage and thus waste-water production will have increased to about 352 per cent. It is quite obvious that, if these figures are true, the problem is growing at an alarming rate.

POLLUTION INDICATORS

What does this increase in waste-water production mean in terms of common indicators of pollution and their quantities? The figures in Table 2 related to 1965 are taken from the values published in that year in the report on pollution in the Detroit River, Michigan waters of Lake Erie, and their tributaries, and the report on Lake Erie and its tributaries. Both reports were undertaken by the us Department of Health, Education and Welfare. It was necessary to estimate figures for the parts of Ontario included in this area; however, they should be reasonably accurate. The total amounts of pollutants in the influent (amount produced) and the total amounts in the effluent (amount reaching the rivers and lakes) are both shown for 1965. Directly below we see the estimated amounts in the influent and effluent for the year 2000.

It should be pointed out that the figures for the effluent in the year 2000 allow for complete secondary treatment of all waste water, both domestic and industrial, and include in their design the latest improvements in phosphate removal, which, accompanied by careful plant supervision, would remove about 60 per cent of it.

The projected figures also consider that by the year 2000 there will be no combined sewers in the region and thence no storm overflows. All in all, the conditions chosen would appear to be optimistic indeed. If the effort brought to bear on the problem during the past thirty-five years is used to extrapolate expected improvements over the next thirty-five years (1965–2000), we will have a far less favourable

TABLE 2

Quantities of certain pollutants in the influents and effluents in the Detroit–Windsor regional area for 1965 and 2000

	Suspended solids		Biochemical (oxygen demand)		Total phosphate		Total nitrogen	
	Influent	Effluent	Influent	Effluent	Influent	Effluent	Influent	Effluent
1965	4,200,000	3,005,000	1,750,000	1,290,000	340,000	310,000	425,000	390,000
2000	12,600,000	1,900,000	5,250,000	685,000	1,020,000	410,000	1,280,000	900,000

Note: All values are in pounds of pollutant per day.

picture in the year 2000 than the one I have indicated. However, I am trying to show that, even if we were to do everything our present technology and resources would allow us to do, we might still not be able to lick the problem by 2000; and the comparison of the quantities of the selected pollutants in the effluents for the years 1965 and 2000 in Table 2 indicate that we will still be in trouble. Although the suspended solids and BOD would be less, the amounts of phosphate and nitrate would still present a problem.

BRIEF LOOK AT A DYING LAKE

Studies by biologists and limnologists indicate that the character of Lake Erie is changing very rapidly. I would call it a dying lake. Now by dying I do not mean devoid of life – quite the contrary. What I do mean is that the life is swinging rapidly towards planktonic forms and water weeds and away from game fish. The water is becoming dirtier; it lacks sufficient dissolved oxygen; it is losing its sparkle; it is heavily laden with bacteria; and it is beginning to give off an offensive smell. In short, it cannot serve many of its established uses without elaborate pretreatment.

The Great Lakes have for centuries been slowly headed in this direction, but man's carelessness has caused this deterioration to accelerate at an almost unbelievable rate. Thus the natural aging of Lake Erie is being hastened by the ever increasing discharges of nutrients such as nitrogen and phosphorus, as well as by a variety of sewage solids from homes and industrial plants. This over-fertilization is called eutrophication. In part this is what happens: the nutrients provide food for algae; the algae live out their life cycle, and when they die they cause a serious biochemical oxygen demand, which is probably the greatest single cause of the rapid depletion in the dissolved oxygen content of Lake Erie waters. To put this in more dramatic terms, it is believed that one pound of phosphate can support one million pounds of algal growth.

Among the problems caused by the increased fertilization and decrease in dissolved oxygen in Lake Erie are greatly decreasing numbers of many of the predominantly clean water forms of aquatic life such as Mayfly nymphs and caddis flies, to mention a few of the most important fish foods for freshwater game fish. This lack of food and dissolved oxygen has placed extreme pressure on the ability of game fish to compete with what we call rough fish for survival. Thus the environment favours the rough fish and is very quickly helping to eliminate the more desirable species of game fish from Lake Erie waters. For example, white fish and pickerel catches are less than 1 per cent of what they were thirty years ago.

A considerable amount of time could be devoted here to cataloguing the many ways in which pollution affects our daily lives, from the loss or at least serious impairment of many of our finest recreational areas, to the taste and odour problems generated by water-purification plants. However, most of us, if we read the newspapers are familiar with these facts and there seems to be no merit in flogging the point. However, I do wish to mention two lesser known points.

1

If the water in the central basin of Lake Erie should lose all of its dissolved oxygen (and the dissolved oxygen level has gone from about five parts per million in 1930 to less than two parts per million in 1964), we would have an anaerobic condition in the central basin, with its production of evil-smelling gas (hydrogen sulphide); but along with this we would have the release of very large amounts of phosphorus from the heavily laden phosphorus-bearing bottom sediments. This process of resolution of phosphorus is very efficient under anaerobic conditions. Since the present phosphate levels in Lake Erie waters are generally below 0.05 parts per million and the algae problem is already very serious, it takes little imagination to visualize what affect the releasing of large amounts of phosphorus from the bottom sediments would have. And make no mistake, the phosphorus is there (reported as high as 1,500 parts per million in some locations), just awaiting a mechanism for its release.

2

Another very significant factor is that we still do not know what harm can be caused to our health by prolonged ingestion of the ever increasing, but as yet trace amounts of a variety of chemicals, all the way from the heavy metals from our electro-plating industries to the detergents we use in the home, and the insecticides we use on our lawns and crops. We know how serious large single doses of these poisons are, but we do not know what prolonged ingestion of traces of them will do. This is an area that is receiving more attention every year and well it might.

POSSIBLE CORRECTIVE STEPS

In order to prevent the boundary waters in our area from becoming more polluted and to effect much needed improvements in their present condition, we must act quickly. The following are my recommendations:

1

Require all new sewage treatment plants to be secondary treatment plants, thus eliminating the possibility of building a primary treatment plant with secondary treatment to be added at a later, often undetermined, date.

2

Set dates for revamping all facilities that are at present inadequate and insist that these facilities be built on a definite schedule.

3

Cease all building of combined sewers and insist on separate sewer systems in all new construction and in replacement of old facilities.

4

Require that all new treatment plants and plans for revamping old ones include in their design facilities for the removal of maximum amounts of phosphate. This is believed to be the best method presently available for controlling the algae problem.

It is obvious that with the available methods of treatment and their efficiency, we will not be able to stay ahead of the problem for long, even if we follow the four recommendations. Table 2, which was prepared on the assumption that the first four recommendations would all be carried out by the year 2000, makes the picture all too plain. Thus it is clear that improvements in treatment methods must be devised and that this must stem from increased support of research programs on the part of government. There can be no room for austerity in this area, for when the public can see and smell the problem as they now can, it is serious. The built-in bonus in such a program is the pool of trained graduate students produced, a commodity at present in short supply and in high demand.

If the figures for the year 2000 are not depressing enough to indicate the seriousness of our situation, we might, if we have the courage, consider the year 2100.

Competition for Land Use in an Affluent Society

MARION CLAWSON

THE COMPETITION FOR LAND and other natural resources in an affluent society has taken a quite different direction from that envisaged by Malthus, Ricardo, and the classical economists. They foresaw problems of providing an adequate food supply as total population rose, with the probable necessity of bringing more land into cultivation. The precise nature of the adjustment that would be needed was foreseen in different ways by different workers, but in the main they thought extra efforts, involving rising costs, would be required to produce more food needed by more people. One such extra effort envisaged by most of them was the bringing into cultivation of poorer and poorer land – land that had not warranted cultivation in an earlier period. Other adjustments were also contemplated.

In so far as they gave it explicit attention, the same general relationship, sometimes more extreme, was believed to exist for minerals and other natural resources. Here, the non-replaceable or exhaustible character of such resources was also given special consideration. It was taken, more or less as an article of faith, that recourse would have to be had to increasingly poorer and more expensive sources of mineral deposits, with resulting higher costs.

These same students foresaw an increased dependency of the industrialized nations upon the less developed ones, as sources of raw materials, including food, fibres, and minerals. Here they were joined by Marx, who also envisioned increased exploitation of colonies for the benefit of the mother country, and increased dependence upon the economically less developed parts of the world. These various writers differed somewhat in the kinds of political and social conclusions they drew, but they were pretty well in agreement as to the trend – rising, for the products of the raw material-producing countries. In modern times this viewpoint has also had its proponents.

In fact, for the past fifty years or so, and at an accelerating pace, the trends have been exactly the opposite – up till now. One may indeed hold that the experience of the past generation or two will prove, in the truly long run, to have been an exception. But the trends and relationships of the past few decades are clear enough, and seem likely to continue for a few more decades, whatever the situation in the more remote future may be.

Agricultural supply, as measured by food products actually produced, has tended to outrun effective agricultural demand, at politically and socially acceptable prices, in the United States and Canada during the past nearly fifty years. Moreover, during that period, except for a few war years, agriculture never produced to the limit of its capacity; at any time, given a little price incentive and the lifting of government controls, agricultural output could have increased considerably in the short run, to say nothing of far larger increases in the long run. The same trends are now showing up in Western Europe, which lags roughly a generation behind us in its modern agricultural revolution. Surpluses, of some commodities at least, are appearing there; and, with the possible exception of feed grains and of products unadaptable to their climate, agricultural self-sufficiency or surplus is in prospect for Western Europe as a whole within a comparatively few years.

Moreover, this mounting agricultural output has been produced, by and large, from fewer acres than formerly. Some soils and land situations have not been well adapted to modern technology, and the land has been abandoned. For instance, in our southeast – the old Cotton Belt – land abandonment in the past fifty years has run at nearly 50 per cent, and cotton has practically disappeared, migrating to more fertile and to more level lands farther west, where mechanization is more practical. Our New England farming areas have experienced land abandonment for a century and longer. These same trends, I believe, have been experienced in Canada.

More dramatic has been the massive reduction of the numbers of people engaged in agriculture. In the US it has been more than half, and is still continuing. It has been caused primarily by the failure of young men and women to stay in agriculture; there has been very little accelerated withdrawal of older farm people. As a result, our farm population is getting older, impressively so in some of our poorer farming areas. Barring some dramatic reversal, the declines in farm and small rural town population will continue at least for the next generation. More than half of all our counties lost population in the 1950s and are still continuing to do so. Many other counties are also losing people in their rural areas but gaining them in their largest town or towns. Canada is facing the same changes, and much of Western Europe is now following the trend or is about to do so.

During the last decade the industrialized countries began to export food in rising volume to the less developed countries of the world. Latin America has experienced a sharp shift from food export to food import, as have several Asian and African countries. The food problems of India are the most publicized and are impressive because it is a very large country.

The terms of trade for raw materials generally have turned against the producing countries, at least in recent years and as compared with what they hoped were normal relationships built up during World War II and the Korean War. Mineral and fuel supplies are generally ample; the problem with petroleum is a more than ample supply to maintain the price structure which producers and processors find desirable. It is precisely because of these trends in terms of trade for raw materials that the less developed countries have been clamoring, through the UN and in other forums, for some form of price or income guarantee or support of these raw materials.

Gunnar Myrdal has argued most persuasively that science and technology have worsened the position of the less developed countries – not only as compared with the advances of the more industrialized ones, but absolutely. He points out that nearly all science and technology have been produced by the advanced industrialized countries and that they have been directed, naturally enough, to the problems of such countries. As examples, he points to the development of artificial rubber and its effect upon the rubber-producing countries, and to the development of plastics which has reduced the dependence upon minerals. He raises the question of what will happen to the coffee-producing nations of the world when we get a satisfactory artificial coffee at a lower price. One need not accept all his conclusions, or get as gloomy about them as he does, to admit that the trend of dependency upon raw material producing countries has been vastly different from what our ancestor economists foresaw.

Since World War ii, we have seen a vast decolonization process, on a scale never previously experienced and never to be repeated since colonies seem to be a thing of the past. Contrary to Marx's expectations, the industrialized mother countries have generally prospered mightily since the loss of their colonies, while the former colonies have frequently experienced major economic difficulties. It seems clear that, under modern conditions, the industrialized nations are economically vastly less dependent on raw materials from the less developed countries than the latter are for industrialized goods and services from the economically advanced countries. The gap between rich and poor countries may indeed be widening, as Myrdal and Barbara Ward among others have argued; at the least, it is not narrowing.

The mounting competition for land in the United States, and in the economically advanced countries generally, is different from the classical model. The effective demand is for land for uses other than agriculture, and it is expressed in different ways.

One of the insistent demands is for more land for urban uses of all kinds, particularly for residential use. More people obviously require more space in which to live. Moreover, were we to have a highly dispersed rural and small-town settlement pattern for our increasing population, still more land would be required, for the small city and town are lavish users of land for residential purposes. The growth of our larger cities has attracted much attention, for it is truly impressive and important. Such cities have swallowed up great chunks of the countryside, to the acute distress of agricultural fundamentalists. In addition to more people, there is a new pattern of urban living developing, that of the suburb, with its single-family house situated on its own plot of land. The density of land use in these new residential areas is nearly always considerably lower than the average density in the older residential districts of the same cities. The private automobile has freed the average person from dependence upon public or mass transport, and has opened up wider horizons for location and made possible the use of more land per family. The change has been great and sometimes dramatic. But it is often overlooked that those parts of the older cities which remain in residential use have often increased in density – apartments have replaced single houses, or larger old houses have been converted into apartments, and crowding has often increased in lower income areas without any change in the physical structures. Moreover, as noted, even the sprawling suburb of today has a higher intensity of residential land use than the small city or town which, in a sense, it replaces.

With very few exceptions, land in real demand for urban uses, particularly for residential, industrial, and commercial uses, has been shifted to those uses, since they have outbid almost every other use in the price they will pay. More impressive to me, in the case of the United States, is the substantial acreage of land around every major city taken out of any other real use and held speculatively idle for ultimate conversion into urban use of some kind. Our data on this point are woefully deficient, but I have estimated that as much land is withdrawn from other uses, kept idle or essentially so while waiting for conversion into urban uses, as is actually used for all urban purposes. The speculative process leads to a bidding-up in price of such land, thus effectively transferring it out of the hands of farmers and other owners; but the same speculative processes seem to make it worthwhile keeping such land idle, so that it can instantly be transferred to some urban developer when he demands it. Thus, for example, erstwhile dairy farms remain idle. Speculative bidding-up of land around our cities is an old American custom – the construction of the Erie Canal led to prices in cities along its route which were not supported by actual urban developments for several decades. In fact, some parts are still undeveloped. I am unfamiliar with Canadian history on this point, but I would expect that some at least of the same processes have taken place.

Transportation, particularly the superhighway and the major airport, has also taken substantial tracts of land in recent years. The total acreages are not so large, compared with the total area for the nation or for a state, but the strategic location of this land has often given it major importance. We are learning painfully that the competition for land between transportation and other uses is most acute within cities; putting a major freeway into and through a city involves not only high money costs but much negotiation and often great disturbance to other land users. I have sometimes talked about the turmoil cost of land-use changes, and this is nowhere better illustrated than in the case of land required for major highways and airports. The requirements are quite specific as to acreage and location, and existing or potential other uses usually must give way. Another transportation use, not quite so demanding as to exact location, is that for the parking lot. If we want people to come into the downtown part of the city, we must provide a place for their cars. While there is some flexibility here, it is much less than for agricultural and residential uses of land. In the United States, at least, the parking lot is often a transitional land use, between the demolishment of an old building and the erection of a new one.

Transportation use of land presents some problems which we have not yet solved. Trying to provide ample freeway capacity at peak periods may be a self-defeating process; the more capacity provided, the greater the use – the traffic jam is merely on a larger scale. It is not fanciful to imagine a city in which all the land given over to freeways and parking lots, with none left for commercial, industrial, residential, and other uses – some may indeed feel that Los Angeles has reached this ultimate extreme. Seriously as the intrusion of the modern highway disrupts established cities, the result is not nearly so bad in some of our cities which are ripe for major reconstruction as it will be in many European cities, where the charm of their older sections is a major economic as well as aesthetic resource. Were it not for the hardship inflicted by the loss of poor housing upon our lowest income groups, one could applaud any program that leads to the levelling of some of our oldest and poorest housing. But the major highway also creates problems for the relatively new and relatively prosperous suburb. Our highway engineers find it increasingly necessary to direct their attention to the economic, social, and political problems of urban land use, which are vastly different from the construction problems studied in their undergraduate classes.

Recreation calls for a mounting use of land and water resources in an affluent and mobile society. The public recreation areas for which we have attendance data show an almost constant rising trend of close to 10 per cent annually. In the case of our national parks, attendance data are available since 1910, and the curve has been steadily upward, again at almost a 10 per cent rate; a slight flattening was apparent in the early 1930s, and a decline took place during World War II when travel was rationed. The same is true for attendance at national forests, state parks, and federal reservoir areas; there is no clear evidence yet of a flattening-out in the rate of growth. I know that in Canada the experience has been similar.

This rising attendance at public recreation areas has been due to several factors – more people, higher real incomes per capita, more leisure, and better transportation facilities have been the major ones. But there have also been more parks or other areas, encompassing more land and using more water. Without an increase in land availability, the mounting demand might have been frustrated; but the demand helped create the climate for increasing the area.

Data on the use of privately owned outdoor recreation areas are less comprehensive. One major development has been the ownership of a second, and even a third, home, primarily for recreation. Summer cottages are an old phenomenon, but their number has increased greatly since the war. Again, the private automobile has been a major factor. More and more people are taking a winter as well as a summer vacation, and the development of seasonal homes in suitable winter recreation areas is marked. The old idea that a family lives in one spot is becoming obsolete. Like the wealthy families of another day, the middle-income families of today and tomorrow will have two or more homes, for seasonal occupancy. We are finding that in a large number of cases what was a seasonal home at one stage of a family's history becomes its major abode in retirement. Many a community which congratulated itself on its summer homes which brought in taxes without demanding such services as schools is now finding that these one-time summer homes have become retirement homes.

Recreational use of land frequently creates intergovernmental problems. People resident in one governmental unit can travel readily, usually by private automobile, to a park or other recreation area provided at public expense in another governmental unit. As much as half the use of some of our state park systems is by residents of other states. Those who reside and pay taxes in one governmental jurisdiction cannot contribute to the cost of public recreation areas in other governmental jurisdictions, except in entrance or other fees for use of the facilities. One of the current issues of recreation policy is the level of such fees or charges, and the extent to which costs of recreation areas should be met out of such revenue. There has been a major change in the thinking of parks and recreation people on this issue in the past decade; at one time most of them were much opposed to raising any significant revenue in this way, whereas today they reluctantly accept it as necessary.

Competition for land and other factors has led to some changes in land prices in the United States which many of us do not regard as healthy. The total value of farm real estate (land and buildings) has about doubled since 1953, a period when total net farm income has been nearly stable. One might think that part of this was an adjustment to a rising trend in general prices. But, while the index of wholesale prices of all commodities has risen modestly during these years, the price level of agricultural commodities has declined slightly, so that it is not clear that movements in general prices have had much influence on farm real estate prices. There has been some fear of inflation, and land has an almost mystical appeal as a hedge against it; to the extent that those who feared general inflation bid up land prices, they helped make rational their own actions. It is hard to know how far inflation and income tax motives have underlain changes in the price of farm real estate. The conversion of land from farm to urban or transportation uses has had some influence. It has affected not only the acreages of land directly involved – which, comparatively, were not very great – but the farmers who received these higher prices used their increased capital to bid up farm prices elsewhere. The two biggest factors, however, have been the economies made possible by the enlargement in farm size, and the federal agricultural programs. Technological changes have enabled one man with the usual farm machines to handle much more cropland in recent years than in earlier days. With his labour supply and the machinery already his, a farmer can manage more land and produce more income; the pressure on him to bid up the price of any available cropland in the neighbourhood is great, and this has undoubtedly been one major impetus to higher farm land prices. He may not be making a very high income, but he is better off with more land than without it. The federal agricultural programs have brought considerable financial reward to landowners, and it is not surprising that such reward has been capitalized into land prices. I have estimated that something like $12–20 billion of the total rise in farm real estate values of $90 billion has been due to these programs.

The great rise in farm real estate prices of the past decade or more have now made it impossible to earn a competitive return on this imputed investment and also pay a return to labour commensurate with what similar workers can earn elsewhere. Many a farmer in the United States today can earn 5 or 6 per cent on the price he could get for his farm if he sold it, but only at the cost of no income at all for his own labour; or he can earn $5,000 or some other not unreasonably high return for his labour, only if he is willing to forego any return on his capital. He cannot have both wages and interest. We have built a farm real estate capitalization structure that will seriously restrict the entry of young men into farming, competitive returns to the factors used in agricultural production, and the adoption of new national programs for agriculture. We have painted ourselves into a corner.

But price rises for land in suburban areas – hopefully

being held to "ripen" for development – have been no less serious. The indexes for such land are not as good as those available for farm land, but every indication is that the price of suburban development land has risen rapidly and steeply since the war. Although we cannot be sure, it seems that the price rise from raw or farm land to developed city lot has been far more than could be accounted for by the investment in public services such as streets and sewers, or than can be explained by savings due to better locational advantages. Some studies suggest that the market process for such land is such as to lead to a spiralling of prices; the owner who might sell can always sit back and wait for a further price rise, while the developer who needs a tract may be under considerable pressure to buy now.

At any rate, the price of building sites in most suburban areas today is a serious obstacle to the building of relatively low priced housing. With lots costing from $2,000 upward, houses will be built that cost from $10,000 upward, a total price of $12,000 or more, into which a typical modern American family will put $4,000 or more of equipment and furnishings, a total investment in housing ranging upward from $16,000. Even with our present relatively high per capita incomes, housing at this level is beyond the means of a very large proportion of younger families, who would be its most logical buyers. If land prices were a third to a half lower, and less expensive houses built, with more modest furnishings, the whole package might be available for somewhat less, and could be brought within reach of large segments of our population which are today priced out of the market for new houses.

I should like to conclude with a few comments on what some economists have begun to call the "externalities" in land values. The value on a residence today in a typical city depends less on what the owner has done to maintain it than on what his neighbours have done – physically and socially. That is, a house in a deteriorating neighbourhood will not command a high price, no matter what its physical condition, whereas a house in a good well-thought-of neighbourhood will be more highly valued, even if it is somewhat neglected and unkempt. The same is true of commercial districts, and of the generally declining downtown area of so many cities. Land takes on value from the activities on other land adjoining it or competing with it. A specific parcel of land has never been self-contained, but the degree and the nature of the relationships are vastly closer and more complicated today than formerly. It is this interrelatedness of land values and of land uses which gives real purpose to community or city planning for land use. The individual works within closely defined limits. The competitive market does not fully recognize these interdependencies.

Transportation and Communications

O. M. SOLANDT

AT PRESENT, the Great Lakes–St. Lawrence area is served by a thoroughly conventional communications and transportation system. It differs from other areas of North America primarily in the relative importance of water transport of freight and especially bulk cargoes during eight or nine months of the year. I will not attempt to describe it, but will merely outline the changes in the various elements that I foresee in the next ten to twenty-five years.

First, let us deal briefly with communications. Communications are of prime importance because, I believe, improvements in this field may have a significant effect on the demand for both freight and passenger transportation. By modern standards, the Great Lakes–St. Lawrence Basin has a first class communications system, consisting of telephones, telex, and a variety of private wire services, plus good radio and television coverage. Nonetheless, there is every evidence from current research that we are on the verge of another revolution in communications. There is so much to be said about the foreseeable developments in this field that it is hard to compress it. Improvements in microwave radio, in coaxial cables, in wave guides, and possibly the use of lasers will vastly increase the total band width available between major centres. The evolution of cheap reliable micro-electronics will make possible the universal digitizing of all information to be transmitted from point to point, whether it be high-speed data transmission, voice, or television. Similarly, developments in micro-electronics will make it economically feasible to have broad-band switching centres capable of automatically routing messages over a fully distributed communications network. Along with this must come a completely new approach to the costing of such services. It seems reasonable to conclude that all of these developments will, sometime within ten to twenty-five years, result in effective and economical transmission of great masses of data and the possibility of business and even personal use of TV. The availability of superior communications media will greatly reduce business travel. It will no longer be necessary to go to another man's office to have one of the eyeball-to-eyeball confrontations that are so popular these days. You will be able to see a lifelike reproduction of the other man's eyeballs in your own office, even though the image has been digitized, processed through several computers, and transmitted over a shared-time communications network. So much for a brief look at the communications of the future.

Now I should like to turn to transportation. I am sure

that the transportation historians of the future will see the middle half of the twentieth century as the age of the automobile.

In the twenty years since World War II, we have seen the evolution in North America of the world's finest system of superhighways. More and more are being built and we are barely keeping pace with the production of new vehicles. However, already in more heavily populated areas such as Los Angeles and San Francisco the situation is becoming critical. A modern highway system uses a great deal of land. In our cities and suburbs, it is already apparent that it does not make sense to take an unlimited percentage of land out of other uses and set it aside for transportation purposes. It is obvious, therefore, that the pressure that has already begun will increase, either for more efficient use of our highways or for other better means of transportation.

Of the many possible ways of achieving a substantial increase in the capacity of existing superhighways, automatic vehicle control seems to be the most promising. It is within the capacity of existing technology to produce reasonably safe and reliable means for controlling automobiles so that they can follow one another at reduced separation at fairly high speed. I do not suggest that this will be easy, but it does appear to be a real possibility if adequate effort is put into the development. I believe that it will be done because it appears, at the moment, to be the best way of increasing the throughput of existing highways while retaining the flexibility and personal convenience of private automobiles as a means of transportation.

However, even before our highways are automated, the expansion of the system in areas of high population density will stop and increased capacity will be sought by high-speed surface public transportation rather than by more highways. This tendency is already apparent and many cities are building subways and beginning to operate new high-speed rail commuter services and improved inter-urban trains. There is now no doubt that the sixties will represent the low point in rail passenger service in North America. But by the end of the decade the upward swing will be apparent. This will begin with the speeding up and improvement of conventional trains. Experience in France and Japan has shown that safe, comfortable, and reliable service at start-to-stop speeds of 100 miles per hour can be achieved within the limits of existing technology. In France, experimental trains exceeded 200 miles an hour some years ago and new experiments in the 150–200 mile an hour range are already under way in the United States. The advent of the gas-turbine as a power plant will make possible lighter and more powerful trains and will help in achieving higher speeds.

Several interesting ideas for reaching even higher operating speeds on or under the ground are now in the stage of active discussion and even early experimentation. Among ideas for surface travel, the hovertrain looks promising. There are several variants of this idea. One, which is in an early stage of development in the United Kingdom, consists of a vehicle not unlike a modern train, but which runs on pads that are lifted a short distance off the track by air pressure. The track itself is a large v-shaped trough which gives both vertical and lateral support to the train. Speeds of at least 300 miles an hour are envisaged as possible and safe for such a vehicle.

When the costs of building a new surface right-of-way, whether for road or railroad, are carefully examined, the engineer immediately wonders about the possibility of going underground to avoid the tremendous expense of grade separations, moving public utilities, etc. Several proposals for high-speed underground transportation have been advanced for the use of the Northeast corridor where conditions are similar to those in the Great Lakes–St. Lawrence heartland but population densities are already somewhat higher. The economics of these proposals are not unpromising even with existing methods of tunnelling. Some engineers hope that, if substantial effort is put into developing cheaper and better methods of tunnelling, it will be possible to reduce costs to a point where underground interurban transportation will be the choice for the future. Speeds of 400 and even 500 miles an hour are envisaged for these underground trains, which could be propelled by air pressure or by linear electric motors and would probably ride on an air cushion.

Whenever a motorist caught in a traffic jam sees a helicopter or plane pass over him, he immediately feels that he would like to take to the air and throw off the shackles of surface transportation. Unfortunately, an analysis of the characteristics of existing air transportation systems merely indicates how unsuitable they are for high-density short-distance travel. At present, cheap, fast, and efficient aircraft require large airfields. Helicopters that can operate with a minimum of ground facilities are slow and expensive and have a low passenger capacity. Clearly, no air-travel system that depends on major airports will be of much use in solving the interurban traffic problems of the Great Lakes–St. Lawrence heartland. Development in both short take-off and landing aircraft and vertical take-off and landing aircraft such as the helicopter give promise of some major improvement in the foreseeable future. For areas where traffic density is not too high, STOL aircraft or helicopters can supply adequate fast and reliable interurban service. Studies for the Northeast corridor have demonstrated this.

I have spoken so far entirely about passenger transportation. The problems of moving freight efficiently in a large area of rapidly increasing population density are also formidable. In the near future this problem will be solved by improvements in the existing system, especially by better integration of road and rail, involving more widespread use of containers and piggy-back. In city centres it will soon be necessary to restrict the hours of delivery for large loads. In some areas these limitations will result in the provision of separate truck routes, possibly at a separate level. The idea of a city centre with one level for pedestrians and another for service vehicles has always appealed to me.

Pipelines will certainly be more widely used. Fuel and/or heat and cooling will be distributed by pipeline even in residential districts.

However, all the obvious improvements that I can foresee will still leave great difficulties in freight transportation to and from urban areas. Business and industry requiring large volumes of ingoing and outgoing freight will be squeezed more and more to the periphery where they can be better served by expressways and railways.

Improved electronic communication will greatly reduce the need for high-speed mail service. The passenger transportation system that I have described could easily handle the small volume of really urgent material other than information. All written material, even newspapers, will be transmitted electronically. There will thus be no need for the development of a special system for the physical transportation of mail at high speed even though improved technology would make this possible.

In conclusion then, I predict that the evolution of surface transportation in the Great Lakes–St. Lawrence heartland will for some years continue the proliferation of expressways. At the same time, there will be steady improvement in suburban and interurban rail passenger service; along with this will go the opening up of heliports or small downtown airports and the growth of interurban air travel over short distances; then, as population densities increase, high-speed trains, hovertrains, and superspeed trains in tunnels will begin to appear. Fortunately, the growth of population in the Eastern megalopolis will probably keep ahead of the Great Lakes megalopolis during this period. As a result, we will be able to profit by their experience and to adopt the modes of transportation known to have been the most successful. Similarly, in the field of communications, it is unlikely that the Great Lakes megalopolis will pioneer many of the developments I have forecast, but it will certainly not lag far behind the Eastern megalopolis in their application.

Special Authorities for the Multistate Megalopolis

MARVIN B. FAST

To THE TITLE OF THIS PAPER I would add "in an international setting," in order to stress that the particular focus is the transboundary aspect of the emerging megalopolis of the Great Lakes area.*

I wish to emphasize too that my purpose is more to explore what may be some of the feasible and useful approaches of the future than to identify the policies and practices of today. I do, however, draw on past experiences in two broad areas, i.e., Canadian–US co-operation across our common boundary and methods used by local governments to adapt themselves to metropolitan growth.

*Views expressed are those of the author alone and are not to be regarded as stating positions of the Federal Water Pollution Control Administration, US Department of the Interior.

This paper has two major parts – a review of a number of ventures in formal co-operation across the boundary shared by Canada and the United States, followed by a discussion of the conclusions emerging from that experience which relate to the problem of developing special authorities for the international megalopolis. Included among these conclusions are two suggested approaches which seem promising in both usefulness and feasibility.

EXPERIENCE IN TRANSBOUNDARY CO-OPERATION

Let us turn first to our common experience in transboundary co-operation, to ascertain, if possible, the governing rules and principles that apply below the level of the national governments – in other words, transboundary co-operation between the provinces (including their local subdivisions) and the states (again including their local units of government).

Transboundary co-operation at the national level in the form of treaties, conventions, and other special agreements is not included, partly because the International Joint Commission is the subject of a separate paper.* A second reason for the exclusion is the assumption that the question of the authorities which will govern the megalopolis is one to which the initial answers will come primarily from the provincial and state governments in our respective systems. It is these governments that today have the authority and responsibility for establishing local units of government. And since this includes the responsibility for facilitating the transition from city and village to metropolis, it is the provinces and states which first will face the challenge of international urbanism and the megalopolis.

A second assumption follows from the first. On the US side of the boundary we are likely to see, as the interna-

*See D. M. Stephens, "The IJC as an Analogy," pp. 100–109.

tional megalopolis develops, an increasing number of proposals to resort to that section of the us Constitution
empowering a state, with the consent of Congress, to enter
into an agreement or compact with a foreign power. For
this reason, it seems desirable to limit the following review
to experience in transboundary co-operation at the level of
the provinces, the states, and their subdivisions.

Among the ventures in transboundary co-operation at
that level, several merit mention:

1

Early in this century a Canadian municipality and a drainage board in North Dakota entered into an agreement
allowing the board to construct certain public works in
Canada. Challenged in the courts, the agreement was held
by a North Dakota court to fall in the category of agreements with a foreign power permitted by the Constitution.
The court also asserted that, because it involved no national
interest, the agreement did not require national consent.

2

About thirty years ago New York State entered into an
agreement with the government of Canada for the acquisition and maintenance of a bridge spanning the international
boundary. The agreement provided for administration of
this facility by the Fort Erie Public Bridge Authority,
through a board appointed jointly by the Governor of New
York and a Canadian authority. This agreement too was
upheld by a state court, even though it lacked the specific
consent of Congress.

3

Instances of transboundary administrative agreements of
a formal nature between provincial and state officials are
not unknown. One such instance is an arrangement between Oregon, Washington, and British Columbia for co-
operation in matters relating to tourist advertising and
information. A second example is the 1931 administrative

agreement on Lake Erie fishing regulations among administrators of four states and the province of Ontario.

Subsequent events in connection with the latter agreement are also worth noting. Breakdown of the agreement led to a proposal in Congress to encourage a formal transboundary compact to regulate fishing in the Great Lakes. This, however, was vetoed by the Department of State, which took the position that it was unable to "concur in the proposal to authorize states to enter into compacts concerning wildlife with contiguous countries or subdivisions thereof." The Department also argued that the "existing method of making treaties constitutes the more appropriate method of regulating this phase of foreign relations."
4

The Northeastern Interstate Forest Fire Prevention Compact, which received the consent of Congress in 1949 without encountering objection from the Department of State, provides that, subject to the consent of Congress, any province contiguous with any member state may become a party to the compact by taking such action as its laws and the laws of Canada may prescribe. Recent developments indicate that provincial membership in this agency is expected in the near future.

Let us turn now to some more recent ventures in transboundary co-operation. The first is the joint program of Ontario Hydro and the Power Authority of the State of New York to develop hydro-electric power at Niagara and on the St. Lawrence. Here again, of course, direct co-operation between these agencies is based on prior agreements between federal authorities in the two countries.

A second recent venture is the attempt of the Great Lakes states to establish the Great Lakes Commission as a transboundary agency. The Commission, an official agency of the eight lake states, functions as a fact-finding and advisory body on Great Lakes water resource problems and programs. Although the Commission has no regulatory or enforcement authority, the intent was to provide the states with an instrument that could effectively influence the government entities responsible for formulating and administrating Great Lakes programs and policies. As originally proposed, the compact creating the Commission provided for membership of the provinces of Ontario and Quebec. It also empowered the Commission to submit its recommendations directly to the government of the United States and the government of Canada, or to either of them. These two proposals quickly brought objections from federal authorities in both countries, with the result that neither feature has ever been implemented and the Commission is restricted to functioning strictly as a us agency.

The latest of the ventures in transboundary co-operation worthy of mention is the International Association of Great Lakes Ports. Consisting of port officials in the Great Lakes cities in both Canada and the United States, the Association is a semi-public organization for exchanging information and for co-operating on matters common to the lake ports. The port officials are municipal employees, but the Association itself does not rest on a statutory basis. Like the International Joint Commission and the Great Lakes Fishery Commission, it functions through two separate national sections.

CONCLUSIONS

What conclusions emerge from these ventures in transboundary cooperation at the state–provincial level? There are seven which seem to be significant for the international megalopolis:

1

Although precedents are not numerous, they are sufficient to support the conclusion that a degree of transboundary co-operation at the state–provincial and local levels may be possible.

2

The co-operative ventures which have succeeded are very modest in nature. Most of them involve single-purpose co-operation, i.e., the performance of a single service or function of government such as the construction of drainage works, acquisition and operation of an international bridge, and production of hydro-electric power.

3

Experience to date is inconclusive with regard to co-operation at the state–provincial and local level for the purpose of jointly studying broad public policy questions and for jointly influencing the makers of public policies. The attempt in the case of the Great Lakes Commission to do this was not successful, but this may have been due to mistakes in the drafting of the compact which could have been avoided. Supporting the view that such co-operation may be achieved, if properly organized, is the success of the International Association of Great Lakes Ports. Although not a governmental agency, it is sufficiently governmental in its membership and the subjects upon which it acts to suggest that a transboundary authority with fact-finding and advisory powers on matters of government concern may not be a complete impossibility.

4

Any transboundary arrangement proposed at the provincial–state levels can be vetoed by higher authorities because of the federal government's supremacy in matters of foreign affairs. Consequently, national consent in the form of specific approval by the federal government is more likely to be a strict requirement as the number of such proposals increases. This means that a claim, such as that in the North Dakota decision that a transboundary agreement involves no national interest and therefore does not require explicit national consent, may be more difficult to sustain in the future.

5

None of the transboundary arrangements mentioned have diminished the powers or altered the structure of any participating government or governmental agency. Taken in conjunction with the fact that we are living in an age of nation states, this suggests that certain methods available within each of our countries for restructuring local governments to meet the needs of metropolitan growth are not feasible in the case of the international megalopolis. These methods include the exercise of extraterritorial jurisdiction by a city, annexation, consolidation of existing governmental units, and metropolitan government or federation. The effectiveness of some of these approaches – as exemplified by the metropolitan governments of Toronto and Winnipeg, the urban county government for Metropolitan Miami, and the consolidated city–county government for Nashville, Tennessee – appears to be impressive. However, since it has not been possible to apply these methods even to strictly domestic metropolitan areas which straddle state or provincial boundaries, it seems doubtful that they can be applied to the more complex problem of transboundary urbanism or megalopolis.

6

One structural device, however, has been successfully applied in the US to the interstate metropolis. This is the device of a special authority such as the Port of New York Authority and the Delaware River Port Authority, which has been employed to meet certain special needs of interstate metropolitan areas. Internationally, the Fort Erie Public Bridge Authority is an excellent example. We may conclude then that the authority device probably should not be excluded from those organizational forms which may have a useful potential in meeting the needs of international urbanisms.

7

Finally, two other methods utilized by local governments to adapt themselves to metropolitan growth may offer feasible and useful ways of achieving needed transboundary co-operation in an international urbanism and megalopolis. Procedural in nature and thus not requiring changes in the structure of existing governments, these methods also offer ways of establishing the transboundary co-operation which is likely to become more urgent and desirable in the future. They have the further advantage of being consistent with, or easily adapted to, the constraints which must control local authorities in a federal system in an age of nation states.

I wish to identify and briefly discuss these additional methods, with the recommendation that each merits further and thoughtful consideration as a method that may be applicable in an international situation. The first method is interlocal contracting and joint local enterprises; the second, voluntary metropolitan area councils.

Contracts between local governments under which one government renders a specific function or service for another and the joint performance by two or more localities of a particular governmental activity or service are common in the United States. The us Advisory Commission on Intergovernmental Relations has endorsed the usefulness of such contract and joint service agreements and recently developed tentative legislation for the states which would authorize local units of government to undertake such co-operative activities. A specific feature of the Interlocal Co-operation Act is its recommendation for an authorization of contracts and joint service agreements between communities in different states. In recommending the Act, the Advisory Commission also noted that, "States having such (i.e., international) boundaries might want to consider whether to devise means for extending the benefits of this suggested act to agreements between their subdivisions and local governments across the international boundary."

An extension of another feature contained in the Act, the provision for state review of such contracts, should adequately protect any national interest that might be involved in a transboundary contract or joint service agreement. By permitting appropriate federal authorities to review the agreement, essential national control over foreign affairs would be preserved.

The growing use in the United States of the second device – the voluntary metropolitan area council – has been described by the Advisory Commission on Intergovernmental Relations as " . . . one of the more significant recent developments in metropolitan areas." The Commission, which has urged the states to encourage the formulation of such councils, has described the council device as follows:

Voluntary "metropolitan councils" are voluntary associations of elected public officials from most or all of the governments of a metropolitan area, formed "to seek a better understanding among the governments and officials in the area, to develop a consensus regarding metropolitan needs, and to promote co-ordinated action in solving their problems." They are intergovernmental agreements for joint conduct of activities in research, planning, and deliberations on issues of area-wide concern.

Although the councils vary with respect to their mode of establishment and membership, they usually have these characteristics: (1) They cut across or embrace several local jurisdictions, and sometimes do not stop at State lines. (2) They are composed of the chief elected officials of the local governments in the area, and sometimes have representation from the State Government. (3) They have no operating functions. Rather, they are forums for discussion, research and recommendation only. Recommendations are made to the constituent governments, or to State legislatures. (4) They are multi-purpose, concerning themselves with many area-wide problems. (5) They employ a full-time staff.

It may be of special interest in the Windsor area to point out that this device for coping with metropolitan area problems originated in Michigan. In 1954, six counties in the southeastern part of the state, which includes the Detroit metropolitan area, established the Supervisors' Inter-County Committee, the pioneering effort in the council movement. At the present time, and as a result of studies by the Metropolitan Fund of Detroit, there is hope for an improved use of this approach through the establishment of a council of all governments in the same region.

Mention should be made of the fact that the staff notes included in the report of the Committee of One Hundred, which developed the proposal for the new Council of Governments, also specifically recommend strengthening Michigan laws authorizing interlocal contracting by permitting agreements across the international boundary.

As a strictly voluntary agency, without regulatory or enforcement authority, the metropolitan council seems especially suited to the international urbanisms of the Great Lakes area, where legal, political, and psychological barriers preclude more drastic organizational forms. If properly structured – i.e., organization in separate but co-operating Canadian and US sections and some control over the methods used to transmit a council's recommendations to higher levels of government – such transboundary councils could usefully serve their component governments without trespassing on national control of foreign affairs.

Canada and the United States justifiably have been proud for many years of the amity and co-operation which have characterized relationships along the border. Megalopolis in the Great Lakes area offers the opportunity for constructive and new demonstrations of harmony.

Physical Planning

WALTER H. BLUCHER

THE SOLE PURPOSE of physical planning and development is to serve the social and economic needs of a people. Perhaps "a major purpose" or "the prime purpose" would be more exact. Certainly, the proper arrangement and utilization of our physical resources serves a useful purpose in itself.

Physical planning, which fails to consider social objectives and needs and the economic potential of an area is indeed sterile planning – a lesson learned during the Depression.

Members of the American Institute of Planners continue to debate the nature of our function or role and how far we should depart from land planning; in Great Britain the same questions arise, involving who should be members of the Town Planning Insitute of Great Britain. In other European countries, and in some Latin American countries, such arguments are purely academic. The planner must have imagination. Only architects have imagination, *ergo* only architects can be town planners! But imagination can be stimulated by listening to Bach and Mozart and reading Shakespeare. It seems to me that 90 per cent of all the buildings designed by architects in all the cities of the world show no imagination!

Those of us concerned with metropolitan planning and government problems find it difficult to learn by experience or from the labours and thinking of others. In 1927 the Pittsburgh area, with 124 municipalities, finally published the report prepared for the Commission to Study Municipal Consolidation in Counties of the Second Class. For some years prior to the completion of the report there had been a feeling on the part of many Pittsburghers that something had to be done to deal with the problems created by the multitude of governmental agencies. An illustrious group had been brought together to study the problems. Among the participants were Dr. Paul Studensky, Secretary of the Committee on Regional Government of the National Municipal League; Professor Thomas H. Reed, Director of the Bureau of Government and Professor of Political Science at the University of Michigan, later to become the outstanding expert on metropolitan problems and solutions, and Dr. Lent D. Upson, Director of the Detroit Bureau of Governmental Research.

What did they find? The same problems that exist in metropolitan areas today. What did they suggest as a solution? A federated form of metropolitan government which would come into being if a majority of the electors voting thereon in the county as a whole, and at least two-thirds of all the electors voting thereon in each of a majority of the cities, boroughs, and townships thereof, voted in the affirmative. These are words that invite disaster, in the eyes of students of government.

What was the purpose of their proposed solution?

It is the purpose of the commission to provide a form of government for all governmental and municipal functions by enlarging and developing the county government as it now is to such a point that where more than one municipality is affected, there can be a genuine, unified force and control to co-ordinate all underlying efforts – not to abolish existing institutions without proper reason, but to multiply their accomplishments by the elimination of duplications, overlaps and conflicts of authority, to the end that their united effort shall result in vastly improved service, with constructive economy and scientific efficiency.

It is realized that in the complex development of our civilization the luxuries of yesterday have become the necessities of today, and that future generations will suffer unbelievable burdens unless the vast possibilities of this industrial giant are considered and future ends anticipated through proper municipal vision, planning, direction and control.

It is further possible, in the judgment of this Commission, to provide by co-operative effort, under the "federated government plan", public utilities, recreational, educational and health advantages here that cannot be obtained elsewhere; and that will result not only in the individual benefit of the people but in the multiplication and diversification of industries in a way not heretofore possible. Skilled men of the various hand and machine crafts are much more likely to be drawn to a center of such development than to the Pittsburgh District of today. Making the whole territory a better place in which to live, to play and to work, a better governed community if possible, where the tax-payer gets a better return for his expenditure – naturally must create conditions that will draw to this great metropolitan area new life, new vigor and new accomplishments.

Reports on the subject of metropolitan problems and solutions have flourished since that time. In fact, we have had a flood of studies and reports in the intervening forty years. There have been some 7,000 of these reports at a rough estimate, but not one of them has stated the problems better (most not as well) nor has anyone yet found a better solution. Toronto's metropolitan government is substantially that recommended for Pittsburgh.

What happened? The solution was voted down. It was obvious at that time that it was practically impossible to get the affirmative vote of two-thirds of all the electors voting in each of a majority of the units of government involved necessary for the creation of a new form of government.

Thomas Reed went on to study a number of communities

with similar problems and to become the outstanding expert in the field. Some years later he was asked to make a study of similar problems in Atlanta and Fulton County, Georgia, and in a monumental report issued in 1938 he offered some solutions:

Flying thief and hurrying pestilence will not stop at municipal boundary lines, but police work and health work as carried on by local governments do. It would be much better, other things being equal, if all existing political lines could be wiped off the map of this section of Georgia and the boundaries of a new consolidated city and county drawn in their stead, embracing all the real Atlanta and a reasonable margin for future growth. There can be no doubt that this would be the best plan. If it could be accomplished by the will of the people and of reasonable and unselfish men it would be done. But such is not possible.

Tom Reed had learned the difficulties of getting people to accept sensible solutions to their common problems. The creation of a metropolitan form of government simply was not possible. That was in 1938 and the picture has not changed to any great degree in the thirty years since. So he offered a second solution – annexation. "The next best thing is annexation. Wholesale annexation at present is impracticable. . . ." So he offered a third solution – the re-allocation of functions and the creation of a Metropolitan Planning Authority. Perhaps, if people would not eliminate their units of government, they might at least plan to deal with their common problems. And yet, it was many years after the report that effective metropolitan planning was inaugurated in the Atlanta metropolitan area.

It was with some amusement that I read in a recent issue of that extraordinary *Atlanta* the following words of Opie L. Shulton, Executive Vice-President of the Atlanta Chamber of Commerce, in an editorial entitled "Beginning to Meddle":

When one meddles it is helpful if he has no qualification in the area in which he meddles. That is why I have chosen today's city as my area of meddling. Nothing that I know of is as mixed-up, complex, and without apparent solution as is today's metropolis.

In the first place, today's city limits make absolutely no sense. City limits began back in the days when walls had to be built around cities to protect them from would-be invaders. The walls of stone have been removed, but another wall has taken the place of the mortar and stone. This new wall, however, doesn't protect the city dweller. Quite the contrary.

Our entire tax structure, for example, was contrived when America was a rural nation. It was designed primarily to punish those centers of iniquity and degradation while protecting the family which produced the food and fiber that kept the nation alive. Things – most of them – have changed. Today the country has become an urban society. Agriculture has become a business venture. The sons and daughters of the farm have gravitated to the cities. Not that this is necessarily good, but it represents the facts of life as they exist. People go where there is an opportunity to earn their livelihood.

So what do we have? An antiquated tax system, a city made up of a conglomeration of little political subdivisions that are completely senseless and useless, each with its own little taxing kingdom but without real purpose.

One of these days there is going to be a complete reorientation of these messes which today pass for cities. We are going to see a reorganization of areas which all are one and the same. Cities are going to be freed from their inability to perform necessary services and to charge for them. People who share in the economic and cultural opportunities of these centers of population are going to begin to pay their share of the freight. In short, cities are going to become political entities that completely encompass those who make it up and who share its opportunities.

Just as a starter, can anyone give me a reasonable excuse for the existence of both Atlanta and Fulton County, when the two share a common destiny?

If it has been impossible in the United States to create metropolitan governments, which do not truly represent a metropolitan area, on other than a county basis (such as Baton Rouge, Louisiana; Nashville and Davidson County, Tennessee; and Miami–Dade County, Florida), and difficult but less impossible to create metropolitan and regional planning agencies covering a number of counties in a single state, it has been equally difficult to create metropolitan and regional planning agencies covering parts of two states.

Legislation for metropolitan planning in the Chicago area was adopted in 1957. It provided specifically that "The Commission created by this Act may cooperate with any planning agency of a sister State contiguous to the area of operation of the Commission to the end that plans for the development of urban areas in such sister State contiguous to the Metropolitan Counties Area may be integrated and coordinated so far as possible with the comprehensive plan and policies adopted by the Commission." This section was provided in the hope that co-operation with the state of Indiana might result, but to date no joint interstate planning agency has come into being. It is hard to recall any area of the United States where the economic problems, problems of air and water pollution, and transportation are as interrelated as those in the Chicago, Illinois–Gary-Calumet, Indiana region which adjoins Chicago.

True, a number of interstate agencies, requiring Congressional approval, have been formed. There is a bi-state agency serving the St. Louis, Missouri–Illinois area, and just recently the states of Missouri and Kansas have created a joint planning agency to serve the Kansas Cities area, where the boundary line between the states is so indefinite that local officials are sometimes puzzled when driving from one state to the other.

And what about Windsor and Detroit? Sarnia and Port Huron? Niagara Falls and Niagara Falls? Nogales, Arizona, and Nogales, Mexico? If the problems of creating interstate agencies are nearly insuperable, how will we deal with the common problems of intercountry communities? Cross the

border from Detroit to Windsor and you get a ticket identifying your automobile which you must turn in when you
leave Canada; and yet there is today a considerable passing
back and forth of trucks carrying automobile parts. Cross
the border from Windsor to Detroit and you may carry
groceries but no citrus fruits and only a limited amount of
Canada's excellent cheese. Crossing the border to work is a
daily happening for many persons living in Windsor, while
many Detroiters have their summer cottages in Canada.
What is the relationship between the market for housing in
Windsor and Detroit? Does one affect the other? Is this
ever discussed by the two countries? We do discuss the
problems of pollution without doing much about it and we
do discuss fish, but where does our discussion begin and
leave off when human beings are involved?

During recent years metropolitan and regional planning
agencies have proliferated like flies in a cow barn. Some of
these were created because of a real understanding that
communities within a metropolitan area are interdependent
and problems will be solved only on a metropolitan or
regional basis. Thus when a metropolitan sewer and drainage study was undertaken for the Detroit metropolitan
area, it was based on an awareness that while Oakland
County might solve its storm drainage problem by dumping
its storm water into the Rouge River, this merely increased
the problem in Wayne County. Others, however, and this
applies to a number created recently, came into being because the federal government has wisely determined that it
will not continue to provide millions of dollars for highways, or money for the acquisition of open space, or assistance in obtaining necessary sewers unless these are dealt
with on a metropolitan basis. The federal government has
finally come to a common sense conclusion that highways
do not stop at city limits but must be designed and built
within the framework of a metropolitan or regional plan.

The most effective metropolitan and regional planning

has come about when the business interests of the community (decision-makers) understand that their business decisions can have a firmer base if there is effective metropolitan or regional planning to show the relationships between transportation, housing, land use, etc. This was the case in the Baltimore area, where it was the community leaders that sponsored the creation of the Baltimore Regional Council. The same type of persons were back of Chicago's metropolitan planning effort. In the Toronto area, the first chairman of Toronto's metropolitan government, a wise and successful business man, depended on his metropolitan planning agency for advice.

A recent article in the *New York Times* told of the difficulties of creating the Metropolitan Regional Council, which serves the New York region and the states of Connecticut, New York, and New Jersey. Certainly, there is no region in the us where the problems are interrelated to a greater extent. Created in 1956, "it could never muster the votes either to obtain legal status as a tri-state agency, thus qualifying for Federal aid, or to establish dues payment." The *New York Times* on October 29, 1966, carried another report headlined "Regional Council Gets New Status," but said in the body of the story, "However, it still lacked the expense-collecting and policy-enforcing powers that some counties that are members had declared objectionable." . . . "The incorporation gives formal status and provides by-laws and rules for the council as a quasi-official organization" and therefore, apparently, it may receive federal grants.

If there are great difficulties in creating an interstate agency for physical planning, how much greater are the problems of creating an effective intercountry agency.

What are the elements that go into the making of a metropolitan or regional plan? A plan is not an end in itself – it is merely a means towards accomplishing a community's goals. But what are the community's goals and how are they determined? By asking people what kind of a community they want? By asking the elected officials what kind of community they believe the community wants? In a democratic system we elect our representatives to make decisions for us, but does that mean they are to determine the nature of the community? Do we canvass the citizens of a community to determine what their goals are? Some will say this is the only democratic way, but unfortunately many questionnaire studies have not proved fruitful because most people have no basis for making decisions of this kind. Goals frequently turn out to be the reverse of gripes. The man dissatisfied with the existing housing situation has as his goal improved housing. The man or woman dissatisfied with schools, or traffic, or transportation, or shopping facilities, or recreation has as his or her goal improved schools or transportation facilities or shopping facilities. Correction of all these problems does not provide a pattern of the future community because they are too narrow. They fail to take into account the social needs of persons who have not expressed themselves or cannot properly express themselves, and they fail to take into account what is possible in the light of the economic base and potential of the area.

But assuming we can reach a consensus on goals, how does the planner proceed? Or does a determination of goals come about after the planner is well along with his studies? Any determination of the physical needs of a community presupposes studies dealing with the following:

A The economy of the region: an analysis of the economic potential of the region and a determination of what problems must be overcome and what action must be taken to develop that potential.

B Population: a determination not only of the characteristics of the present population and the customary studies of migration, household composition, income, and education, but a determination of the capabilities for employment, handicaps to employment, training required, etc.

c Social problems: characteristics of the underprivileged and handicapped for whatever reason; social services required, housing required, training required, subsidies required, etc.

d Housing: related to the proper housing of all sectors of the population.

e Transportation: taking into account all forms of transportation, whether by water, rail, highway, or pipeline, and dealing particularly with opportunities of providing transportation by methods other than highways. To what extent could mass transportation effectively move people? What must we do to encourage people to walk? How many children could bicycle to school instead of being bussed or chauffeured by their parents if there were safe bicycle paths?

f Open space and agriculture: what open space should be acquired for recreation? What open space should be reserved because it is not suitable for proper development? What should we do to preserve agriculture and ensure that the best agricultural lands remain in that use and come into urban use only after less desirable agricultural lands have been urbanized?

g Water supply and waste disposal.

h Land use and its proper development going beyond what has been set forth above – in other words, the total related picture.

i Historical aspects; aesthetics, cultural facilities, educational facilities.

j Recreation in all its forms including that required for the increasing number of elderly persons.

k Urban renewal: broadly defined to take into account all actions public and private required to build the desired community.

l Methods of implementation: financing the building

of a community, including methods of taxation and sources of funds.

Obviously, what I have set forth above is the sketchiest outline of a program for the physical development of a community. I have attempted to show that physical planning standing alone or a study of physical characteristics will not provide any solution of the problems that beset human beings, most of whom live in urban areas.

You will note that I have not used the word "megalopolis" in this paper. I do not like the word. It reminds me too much of "megalomania," and I fear that the one will lead to the other. I am not at all certain that the overcrowded, congested condition that some people foresee for megalopolis is either desirable or necessary. If physical planning has any meaning at all, it means that we can exercise some control over our environment – that is if we consider the nature of our environment important to human beings.

But back to intercountry planning. Some years ago it was seriously proposed that Detroit's airport be located on the Canadian side of the river at a location within easy reach of the Ambassador Bridge. It was even proposed that there be a special fenced highway leading from the airport to the bridge, to facilitate customs and immigration services. The idea was abandoned, and one of the principal reasons given was the impossibility of establishing suitable inter-country arrangements for its operation.

Mr. Fast has discussed possible arrangements for inter-country activities. I would suggest another method. First, there must be effective and realistic planning at the local and regional level on both sides of the border. There is no reason why the regional planning agency in the Detroit area should not take into account, in its planning, those factors on the Canadian side which affect Detroit's planning; and there is equally no reason why the regional planning agency on the Windsor side should not take into account in its planning those factors from the us side which affect its planning. I would say that failure on the part of either or both to take those factors into account would make for incomplete planning. Then, there should be a high degree of co-operation between the planning agencies on both sides of the border. This applies as well for Sarnia and Port Huron, Niagara Falls and Niagara Falls. (Such planning is now under way between the us and Mexico.) We have not yet begun to scratch the surface to determine how much can be accomplished through co-operative effort, without formal legal arrangements.

True, our aim is to formulate a physical environment where human beings can live happily in a world where happiness is rare. Given an ideal physical environment where all the houses are homes, where transportation facilities are ideal, where schools meet the demands of every facet of the population, we still do not have an ideal community if the air is polluted, if the rivers are dirty, if some people are underprivileged or uneducated, if health and medical facilities are not available to all who need them, if hostilities exist betwen segments of the population. The proper physical setting will help but we must strive to use that physical setting only as the foundation for a community where people can live a full life as human beings.

The IJC as an Analogy

D. M. STEPHENS

THE PURPOSE OF THIS PAPER is to examine the possibility that in the Boundary Waters Treaty of 1909, in the body of principle that is set out in that Treaty, in the International Joint

Commission established by the Treaty, in the mechanisms that are provided for in the Treaty, and in the procedures that have been evolved by the International Joint Commission, there may be analogies that would be useful in coping with problems that arise from the growing international megalopolis.

Most of us would agree that the welfare and happiness of individual members of a family will be affected, sometimes for the better and sometimes for the worse, by the activities and the behaviour of other members of that family. In a somewhat similar way, one community of people can by its actions and its behaviour affect the welfare and happiness of another community of people.

Just as with a family, it would seem that one community of people is more affected by the actions and behaviour of another community if the two are close together, than if they are far apart. It would follow then that as communities, and particularly urban communities, grow and spread and occupy more and more space, they are likely to become contiguous, and in this way to give rise to a situation where the welfare and happiness of one community is increasingly affected by the activities and behaviour of other contiguous communities. This is particularly true when a community occupies open spaces that were once available, as sanctuaries, for another community; or as one community, by its waste disposal practices pollutes what had earlier been a satisfactory supply of potable water for the other; or as the industries of one community pollute the air that the people of another community must breathe.

But these intercommunity interactions need not, of course, be all adverse. In many cases neighbouring communities, acting in concert toward agreed objectives, have been able to achieve much more than one community acting alone could have done. Better water supplies, better waste disposal facilities, better educational institutions,

better cultural opportunities, better transportation facilities, and many other advantages have often resulted from
joint community action.

One of the challenges confronting us, as we witness the
increasing tendency toward contiguity between communities that were once separate and distinct, is how to reduce
the disadvantageous aspects of this closer environment and
how to increase or exploit more fully its advantages. And
because there is a strong human aversion to the denial of
initiative and to the loss of identity, we should concern ourselves with the accomplishment of these other purposes
with the least sacrifice of community initiative and identity.

Many aspects of this problem take on added complexity
and perhaps increased importance when these separate but
closely contiguous communities are governed by the laws
of different legislatures; and still more so when these separate but contiguous communities are parts of different
nations.

It is in some such context as this that I propose to discuss
certain analogies between the circumstances arising from
the international megalopolis and some of the circumstances which resulted in the Boundary Waters Treaty of
1909. In this context also I should like to canvass the possibility that the IJC and the procedures developed by it over
the years may have some relevance for the devising of
new mechanisms to deal with the problems of the international megalopolis.

The Treaty and its mechanisms, particularly the IJC, have
proved to be very useful in the resolution of a great number
and a great variety of intercommunity and international
problems. Of the many aspects of the Boundary Waters
Treaty, the Commission, and its procedures that might be
revelant to the present discussion, there are six that warrant
brief mention.

First, the circumstances that brought about the Treaty

were somewhat analogous to the circumstances of the so-called international megalopolis. In at least one field, the use of surface waters, of common interest to Canada and the United States, activities and/or behaviour in one country were already more than fifty years ago beginning to have an effect upon the interests of people in the other country. This was so with respect to the use of water at Niagara for power purposes, and to the use of the waters of the Milk and St. Mary rivers for irrigation purposes. The Boundary Waters Treaty spelled out the rules which were agreed upon in these cases.

Second, the two countries agreed that in the use of surface waters that were of common interest to the two countries or communities further problems could arise in the future, and they agreed upon a series of principles which would govern future activities and behaviour in these fields. After describing the waters that were to be regarded as of common or mutual interest, the authors of the Treaty proceeded to spell out a series of agreed principles:

That each country should have equal and similar rights in the use of these waters.

That navigation in these waters should be free and open to the vessels of both countries.

That neither country would permit waters in one country to be polluted to the injury of health or property in the other.

That neither would permit obstructions in water courses such as would alter levels or flows at the boundary other than after authorization in a manner set out in the Treaty.

That since some uses of water might be incompatible with others, certain uses should not be permitted to interfere with certain other uses. Hence a series of priorities in water use were agreed upon.

This early agreement between the two nations as to the basic principles or guidelines has been of great assistance in dealing with subsequent problems, and it may have relevance to the international aspects of the megalopolis.

Third, and again because the two countries or communities contemplated a long life in close proximity and anticipated that future problems with regard to surface waters would no doubt arise, they created the machinery through which such problems might be dealt with. The particular mechanism selected was the International Joint Commission. The parties to the Treaty agreed "to establish and maintain an International Joint Commission of the United States and Canada composed of six commissioners, three on the part of each country." The assumption made in the Boundary Waters Treaty that as between dynamic communities problems will also be dynamic, was sound for water matters and could be valid for intercommunity affairs as well.

Fourth, the procedures through which the IJC addresses itself to such problems as may come before it should be of particular interest in the context of the international megalopolis.

Almost routinely, in recent years, when the two governments refer a matter to the International Joint Commission, they inform the Commission at the time the reference is made that it may call upon members of the permanent services of the two governments for information and specialized assistance. And almost routinely also, in recent years, the Commission, upon receiving a reference, will establish an advisory board or boards.

These boards are usually made up of people who have specialized knowledge of the particular subject matter referred to the Commission. Frequently, in order to get adequate representation on its boards or other working groups, the Commission will draw from the specialized services of provinces, states, or local government services, and from universities. In this way groups of people are put to work who represent not only the two nations, but provinces, states and municipalities, as well as the relevant disciplines and specialized fields.

Once the boards and work groups have been established and their terms of reference formulated, the Commission frequently arranges for a series of preliminary public hearings to which all parties interested in the particular problem are invited to come and be heard.

Usually, the first assignment of the boards and work groups, after the preliminary hearings, is to assemble all the relevant known facts, to ascertain the areas with respect to which further facts are necessary, and to recommend to the Commission suitable programs through which necessary additional information can be obtained and co-ordinated.

The process through which appropriately trained people from the two countries, from other levels of government, gather together a body of agreed factual material is an exceedingly useful one, and helps to achieve a maximum of common ground. The "feed back" from the officials involved in the actual studies to the responsible departments of government in the two countries and in other levels of government helps to establish a useful rapport.

Still later, the Commission may ask its board to indicate appropriate principles to be applied to the facts obtained, and this exercise contributes to objectivity in attitudes and the further extension of "common ground" and the development of suitable and acceptable solutions.

The board subsequently produces a report of its findings and sometimes of its recommendations to the Commission. At this stage it is customary for the Commission to arrange for distribution of the board's report, not only to the two federal governments but to state and provincial governments, and to all interested parties. After the report of the board is made available, public hearings are held when all those interested are given a convenient opportunity to be heard.

Following such public hearings, the Commission has

before it not only the facts, the applicable principles, the views of its experts, but the transcripts of all the views expressed. After careful study of this material and much discussion between the six commissioners, a report is drafted and forwarded to the two governments.

Fifth, the Boundary Waters Treaty was framed to provide a variety of roles for the IJC, depending upon the nature of the problem or problems that might arise between the two countries in the fields encompassed by the Treaty. A certain body of subject matter, dealing essentially with works that might affect the levels or flows of boundary waters, was permanently referred to the Commission. The Treaty also provided, under Article IX, that "any other questions or matters of difference arising between them [the two countries] involving the rights, obligations, or interests of either in relation to the other or to the inhabitants of the other, along the common frontier . . . shall be referred from time to time to the International Joint Comission for examination and report, whenever either . . . Government . . . shall request that such questions . . . be so referred." Reports under this article are advisory only and shall not "have the character of an arbitral award."

Under Article X of the Treaty, questions could be referred to the Commission by the two governments, each with its appropriate consent, for a determination, or in effect for an arbitral award. This section has not been employed.

On the other hand, several scores of cases have been referred to the Commission under Article IX for examination and advisory report. The fact that so many such cases have been referred to the IJC and that the references have had to do with a great variety of matters provides some evidence of the usefulness of the IJC and its procedures.

It is worth noting that some of the problems arising from the growing international megalopolis, and perhaps even most of them, could conceivably fall within the ambit of the language of Article ix of the Treaty as being "questions ... involving the ... interests of ... the inhabitants ... along the common frontier." To the extent that this is so, the Boundary Waters Treaty provides not only a useful analogy, but even a potential mechanism.

Sixth, and finally, if the ijc has been successful in dealing with a wide variety of intercommunity problems on an international basis – and it has been successful – that success should in all fairness be attributed primarily to the wisdom and the prescience of the authors of the Treaty. Beyond this I suggest that there are at least three basic reasons for the particular genius of the ijc as an international institution.

First, the Commission is a unitary body. It is not a normal instrument of diplomacy or of negotiation. The six commissioners act as a unit: all are exposed to all of the facts, all of the viewpoints, all of the argument, and in concert arrive at conclusions.

Secondly, solutions to these intercommunity problems have been found which permitted progress to be made towards agreed objectives, notwithstanding marked differences in constitutional arrangements, and a lack of parallelism as to where among various levels of government in the two countries jurisdiction in various fields might lie. And sometimes, as was the case in the reference on vessel smoke-pollution in the nearby narrow waters of the Detroit River, once objectives were agreed upon, marked progress towards their achievement was accomplished by concerted voluntary action, even while the complex jurisdictional problems were being resolved.

The third reason for the particular genius of the Commission lies in the fact that its fundamental purpose is to arrive at agreed objectives. Towards this end the Commission places great weight upon its public hearings. It surrounds itself with experts to ensure that the objectives are practicable and attainable. The Commission does not regard its role as essentially administrative. It is not a mechanism for management. It does not have, nor should it have, enforcement functions. But working towards the development of common objectives, it makes a very real contribution to better management by other appropriate authorities. Management "by objective" is much talked of these days. But for many years now IJC has been contributing to better management in a number of fields of interest to the inhabitants of the two countries by helping to formulate, concert, and agree upon practicable objectives.

The relevance of the Boundary Waters Treaty, in the IJC and in their procedures, to the problems of the growing international megalopolis can be summed up as follows:

1
The circumstances lying behind the formation of the Boundary Waters Treaty have points of similarity with the circumstances of the international megalopolis.

2
As new problems arise, it is helpful if we can agree upon principles that would have application in their solution.

3
The tidying up of outstanding problems and the making of provision for the resolution of such problems as arise in the future has much to commend it.

4
The procedures of the IJC and the manner in which they have facilitated the reaching of common objectives would make a useful "case study" in the context of the international megalopolis.

5
The terms of the Boundary Waters Treaty could perhaps comprehend at least some of the problems which will arise from the phenomenon of the international megalopolis, and hence something in the way of a mechanism may be already available.

6

Finally, in the attempts to find suitable mechanisms for dealing with the problems of the growing international megalopolis, means must be sought through which objectives can be agreed upon and co-ordinated. Many of our existing agencies are fully competent to work towards and to achieve practicable objectives if we can but agree upon what these objectives should be. You may or may not share my own scepticism about the need for, or the probable effectiveness of new, all-powerful, supranational agencies or authorities such as are sometimes proposed when new international problems present themselves.

3. HISTORY AND THE FUTURE

The Great Lakes and the International Megalopolis

HARLAN H. HATCHER

No PART OF MY CAREER has given me more enjoyment than that devoted to the Great Lakes, the impressive heartland of the North American continent. Among other things, I once did what is known in the motion-picture trade as a treatment – a scenario script – under the title "Border Without Vehemence." This project dramatically brought to light the extraordinary fact of two nations separated only by an imaginary border fence, living without hostilities for one hundred and fifty years. Indeed, the only fortresses are now museums for the pleasure of tourists and for the instruction of youth concerning an era that is past. The task and the opportunity of our age is not to refortify the border, but to bridge it for the benefit of both countries. "Something there is that doesn't love a wall, that sends the frozen ground-swell under it, and spills the upper boulders in the sun" (Robert Frost, *Mending Wall*). Dr. Doxiadis' sweeping study of the area may well be such a groundswell. We may yet see international airports, highways, model city developments around Windsor and Sarnia, Port Huron, Mt. Clemens, and Detroit, with linkages as natural and easy as the Windsor Tunnel, the Ambassador and the Blue Water bridges, or the exchange of electric power and the joint use of the Great Lakes–St. Lawrence Seaway. But those details are for Dr. Doxiadis and his professional staff to expound and formulate recommendations.

There are, however, a few observations that seem pertinent and important to the understanding and the perspective of our citizens, if they are to make decisions that will influence the future. The first is the fascinating drama of discovery, of settlement, and of development. This drama is still unfolding, though in different ways and in different dimensions. It is worth just a moment to reflect on the most stimulating chapter in the history of the North American continent. Foot by foot, mile by mile, year after year, the early explorers wedged deeper and deeper into this wilderness, gradually uncovering what lay behind the next bend in the river. These men were goaded by the glittering promises of a route to the Orient, and by the sleek furs of millions of woodland animals. Once the land had been tamed, and the value of its timber and ores had been realized, the Great Lakes area became the scene of such massive productive activity that it now overwhelms the imagination.

Let us visualize the map in the year 1534 and imagine the 2,000 miles of waterway of the St. Lawrence and the Great Lakes unknown at that time. The intrepid young Jacques Cartier is making his way slowly and painfully up the St. Lawrence, and finally arrives at Montreal in the year 1535, led on by Indian tales of the many thundering waterfalls on these immense inland seas. Arrived at the site of Montreal, he read a chapter from the Gospel according to St. John to the Indians assembled there, and then climbed to the top of Mount Royal, where he saw the Laurentian Mountains off to the north and the Adirondacks of New York State to the south. Beckoning him westward were the Lachine Rapids sparkling in the sun. This obviously was the road to Cathay and to the wealth of China. One of the choice bits of our nomenclature records this moment for all time in the name "China Rapids."

Sixty-eight years go by, and nothing has been done. Then

Champlain follows much the same dream and in one of those decisions which alter the fate of a continent, he decided to extend the empire by moving due west, paddling and portaging up the difficult Ottawa River, Lake Nipissing, and finally over to Lake Huron. Had he travelled south southwest instead, he might have established a pattern that could have kept the Great Lakes in French hands. Instead, he left the easier southern route along Lake Erie to the fierce Iroquois Indians who barred his way. Later it fell to the British.

I have followed Champlain's trail and read his journals over and over again, watching him struggle up the Ottawa to the site of the city that now bears the river's name, then portaging over those difficult routes until he came to the French River. Finally, in July 1615, he got his first view of the Upper Great Lakes region. Unfortunately, this eminent geographer did not write a glowing account in his journals of the magnificence of this expansive water. Instead he has an interesting paragraph on the fact that there were a lot of fine pumpkins to be found. At that point he turned south and came back through the maze of islands in eastern Georgian Bay, and looped back across Huron County to Montreal, thus completing his view of the Great Lakes.

In 1634 the first full-fledged expedition, under the command of Champlain's gifted young lieutenant Jean Nicolet, set out to search for China once more. One of the most fascinating and dramatic chapters of this whole period of exploration is the spectacle of this magnificent flotilla sailing across Georgian Bay, making the first journey through the beauty of the Straits of Mackinac. Just when he was about to land in the Orient, with all its richness, Nicolet landed instead in an onion patch, with Indians all about him. This was the site of Green Bay – the Green Bay Packers were not there, but the Winnipago Indians were. Nicolet now had to begin his long trek home, and re-establish his mental concept of the great North American continent. In

1660 two amazing young fur-traders, Radisson and Chouard (Groseilliers), paddled through the Straits, entered Green Bay, went as far west as the Mississippi, roamed around Lake Michigan, came back through the Straits, and went up to the Soo and Lake Superior. When they returned to Montreal, they had sixty canoes filled with furs valued at 200,000 livres. This was greater wealth than had been envisioned from a journey to the Orient. These furs, plus the souls of the Indians that needed saving by the missionaries of the Church, were wealth indeed. Concern for the souls of these Indians caused young Frenchmen to press farther and farther inland. And between the major explorations and expeditions, there were hundreds of lesser journeys of traders, and of the self-sacrificing Jesuit priests, who penetrated the area and brought back knowledge of the Great Lakes region. They finally reached St. Ignace and Michilimackinac in 1670. Later, British engineers built the fortress which can still be seen on Mackinaw Island. The last gap in the exploration and opening up of this great region was closed when in 1669–79 the explorers made their way down the Detroit River. Jolliet, after rescuing an Indian prisoner from the stake at the Soo, was brought to this region by the grateful native, who took him through the Detroit River and down Lake Erie.

From this brief outline, which portrays adventurous men seeking the Orient and finding instead furs and a magnificent countryside, we move on to the Great Lakes region in the first period of its productivity. For a hundred years furs were the cash crop of the Great Lakes. By 1780 there were fleets of fifty to sixty canoes roaming the Detroit area. Six million pelts were taken annually to the trading base of John Jacob Astor. This hive of activity lasted for several decades, reaching its peak in the 1820s. What happened to it? Basically people, and the discovery of the need for lumber. This precipitated the second great epic in our region. The axe of the lumberman, followed by the pick of the miner, became the tool that opened up and cleared the great wilderness. Within two decades, busy settlers pushed the fur traders to the more remote regions. In 1854, there were sixty-one lumber mills in the whole of the Great Lakes region. By 1872 there were 1,500 mills, and by 1881 the State of Michigan alone, while trying to rebuild Chicago and to help build Buffalo, shipped out enough lumber to fill 2,500 miles of freight cars. Buffalo became one of the leading lumber ports of the world, closely followed by others along the Great Lakes.

Then came mining. From 1830 to 1840, there were just two dividend-paying copper mines. Following the opening up of the Calumet and Hecla mines in its upper peninsula, Michigan served as the only source of copper until the mines in the West were opened in the 1880s. Mining of iron ore started in 1844–5, and the first companies in Marquette County had to carry their ore down the Indian trails by wagon. It was twelve miles to the water's edge. Here the ore was loaded aboard ships that came through the Detroit River, which at low water could only accommodate ships with draughts up to about seven feet. Wheelbarrows and plank roads! Such were the primitive beginnings of today's great system of ore loading, unloading, and transport which made the Great Lakes of such vital importance.

The dominant theme of this report is vastness. The size of the lakes themselves, the lands they drain, the scope of John Jacob Astor's fur trade, the broad belts of white pine and hardwood stripped from seven states and two provinces, millions of tons of iron ore scooped from five mountain ranges, the immensity of the grain elevators and ore docks, the cavernous ships to carry these cargoes – indeed, it is a tremendous panorama.

There was one other important cargo – people. A flood of immigrants, lured by the promises of the West, poured through the Mohawk Valley to Buffalo. Passenger ships carried them from Buffalo to Detroit, Chicago, and Milwaukee, and to the various ports of Canada. Ninety such ships docked at Detroit alone in May 1838. Swedes, Finns, Norwegians, Germans, Irish, and Poles – in all, twenty-one dominant nationalities filled the area. Enclaves still remain intact around the Great Lakes on both sides of the border, and their united efforts, unaffected by national borders, have helped the two nations to develop in peace. As trade flourished, word of the "land of opportunity" spread around the world. The Great Lakes cities grew apace: Buffalo, Detroit, Cleveland, Chicago, Milwaukee on the American side; Montreal, Quebec, Toronto, Hamilton, and Windsor, on the Canadian. By 1906 each of these cities held a prominent position. If one were to blot out the cities which rim the Great Lakes, our nations would still be strong, but the great throbbing central portion would be depleted. These cities reach back from the waterfront deep into the land, symbolizing the energy of the men and women who live in them. They stand out as centres of industry, education, art, sociology, politics, and religion. Each has an individual spirit, an individual achievement. We have, however, been prodigal, though not overly wanton or malicious, in our use and our waste of this magnificent heritage of natural resources, and of our potentially beautiful and supportive environment. We are now trying, with some success, to recover from the destruction and waste of our timber lands. We are making progress in utilizing the waste of our iron mines, and in re-using our abused lands. The crisis of our fresh water supply and of air and water pollution is just beginning to capture our attention.

Let us go back some twenty years. At that time, I was engaged in what might be called aerial research on several books, in particular one on Lake Erie. Flying over Lake Erie, especially after an early spring storm or flood, the relatively short rivers that break the shoreline on both sides

of the border everywhere resembled great fingers stained
yellow and brown and red reaching out into the once lovely
lake. Corrosion, sewage, and industrial waste pour into one
of our greatest assets: that is pollution!

Since that time the crisis has mounted, and Lake Erie
is now so polluted that a government official, in recently
announcing plans for federal–state co-operation, said: "If
we can recover Lake Erie, we can save anything." Two million, six thousand tons of filth, sewage, municipal waste,
and chemicals pour into it from the Detroit River alone
every year. In the great central basin of the lake, covering
more than one-fourth of its total area, the amount of dissolved oxygen in the water has been decreased by more
than one-half and some portions have none at all. Lake Erie
is dead; life can no longer exist in it. This is the story of one
of our prime assets. Perhaps you have asked the question:
how did such an unwelcome condition in this magnificent
heartland of America come about so abruptly? In answer,
let us say that it is a by-product of our manufacturing, of
always growing bigger if not better, and of our inadequate
understanding of population growth, land utilization, and
urban development. It was hastened, too, by the impact of
an explosive population. Man is at fault, erecting his forty-
storey office buildings side by side, block by block, in our
cities; using his beautiful waterfronts strictly for utility; and
discarding the waste products of his endeavour into a prime
source of his wealth.

Our concern in this conference has been the woeful condition of our expanding cities in this kind of environment.
We ask ourselves the question: what can we do about it?

A major cause of this condition has been the relentless
shift of people from country to town. In Canada at the turn
of the century the population was 63 per cent rural and
37 per cent urban. By 1951, exactly fifty years later, by a
curious coincidence, those figures were reversed. The re-

versal has continued sharply into the sixties, and the figures
are now close to 75 and 25 per cent. When this fact is combined with a population growth from five to nineteen million, the impact is very great indeed. The same thing, on a
larger scale, has happened in the United States.

Between 1951 and 1961 the population of the metropolitan areas in Canada increased by over 60 per cent. There
are many reasons for this. Basically, the first is the movement of manufacturing jobs from the centres of urban
population since World War I; and the second is the growing interest and concern of the middle class in seeking
space, privacy, and modern housing. This has often created
slum areas in former residential districts while stimulating
building booms in the suburbs, with all the resulting im-
provisation of expressways, utilities, shopping centres,
schools, hospitals, and churches that erase or engulf the
space and the privacy that lured people there in the first
place. The cities are overburdened; their utilities hopelessly
obsolete. They have massive investments in these out-
moded facilities, which seemed well designed for the booming 1880s and 90s and to the upsurge of the first quarter of
this century, when the basic commitments and investments
for water, sewers, schools, street patterns, subways or surface transportation were made. But as people flooded into
the cities and overflowed them, the basic systems were
extended, and sometimes improved. But a crisis stage has
now been reached. The centre is being transformed into a
core area of financial, service, and cultural districts requiring massive transportation to and from the suburbs. This
has caused growing congestion, air pollution, water, sewage, and waste disposal problems. It has so far been next to
impossible to improve the old investment sufficiently or to
begin anew. This is especially ironic, or rather frustrating,
when one considers that we now have the advance knowledge and the brilliant technology required to build and

equip cities adequate for our present needs, more attractive
and able to support, rather than intensify, the living in
them.

Let us keep in mind that urbanization is growing. The
city is here to stay. It is and will continue to be our inescap-
able environment. What we make of it is our responsibility,
and that is quite a challenge. Mankind over the centuries
has indicated that he finds gregarious life, in urban environ-
ments, supportive and more desirable than rural withdrawal. Wordsworth, the greatest of all the nature lovers,
wrote the best of London poems, standing at early morning
on Westminster Bridge. This from the man who drew inspiration from the vernal woods, and espoused the relationship of man to nature. Yet he says:

> Earth has not anything to show more fair:
> . . .
> This City now doth, like a garment, wear
> The beauty of the morning; silent, bare,
> Ships, towers, domes, theatres, and temples lie
> Open unto the fields and to the sky;
> All bright and glittering in the smokeless air.

Johnson abounds in praise for London. It is all summed up
in a famous passage I should like to draw to your attention.
In 1777, Jamie Boswell was contemplating leaving the old
family estate in Scotland and taking up residence in London. He was worried that he would lose the sense of ex-
quisite zest which the city gave him after only brief visits.
So he asked Dr. Johnson what he ought to do about it. And
Johnson made this famous remark: "Sir, why, sir, you find
no man at all intellectual, who is willing to leave London.
No, sir, when a man is tired of London, he is tired of life,
for there is in London, all that life can afford." If all that
life is going to afford is in this Great Lakes region, then we
had better do something to make it worthwhile.

Canada and the United States must join in finding a way

to better living conditions. One of Canada's distinguished men has pointed out that the oldest and the most tenacious tradition in the Canadian communal memory centres around the determination not to become Americans. This is the one tradition in which English-Canadians and French-Canadians have been wholeheartedly united. French Canadians know the acid of the American melting-pot. Ontario was settled by Americans who rejected the Revolution in order to remain faithful British subjects. But all forces are against ultimate success in retaining artificial differences. Under similar conditions of life, similar human reactions will occur.

Industrialization, knowledge, education, economics, geography, history, technology; all modify evolution, and blur the differences which we try to preserve. This is obviously happening in a dramatic way all over the world. I still remember arriving after midnight in Moscow in April 1959. People were practising for May Day in Red Square. Flashing up in the sky was a great red neon sign. I asked my interpreter what it said, and he replied: "Sir, that says: 'Save your money at 3 per cent.' "

Each city and each nation has its own problems, but they are similar. When the city of Cleveland turned a central slum area that once was prosperous into a new university campus, the dislocated people had nowhere to go, but elsewhere in the tense and overcrowded district, which immediately exploded into violent frustrations. This is an example of our present incapacity to use our knowledge for urban development and redevelopment. This overcrowded district of Cleveland lies in the shadow of the magnificent Erieview development, south of the improving lakeshore, which was once a dump, and on the edge of an institution of higher learning, but it ranks with Watts and Harlem as one of the heartbreaking situations in the growth and decay of cities.

However, progress is being made, as evidenced by the Seaway, the lakeshore at Cleveland, Detroit, Milwaukee, Chicago, and now this ambitious and comprehensive study of a region whose development can still be directed and controlled. It is leading more and more decision-making groups to think in larger and more co-operative terms of the future into which the present decisions are taking us on both sides of the border. We are already far behind, but there is still time. Not only should we have borders without vehemence, but an environment without borders might be worth our efforts.

Problems of Megalopolis

JOHN ROBARTS

APART FROM THE INTERNATIONAL APPROACH, the problems discussed at this conference are substantially those arising from urban growth wherever it may occur. These, of course, are the familiar problems of water and power, competition for land use, transportation and communication, the planning process, the administrative framework, and co-operation in its widest sense.

I have had to choose between two approaches. The first was to give a broad and comprehensive treatment of Ontario's position with respect to planning for urban development; the second, of a more restrictive nature, to deal with but one aspect of the total problem. I decided in favour of the latter, largely from a desire to establish firmly that it is possible to make substantial progress in urgent sectors of the urban development problem, even though the exceedingly difficult task of constructing an overall plan is far from complete.

Indeed, in my judgment, the work of the planner is never done. There is now, and will continue to be, a measure of uncertainty in forecasting the development process. While the work of the planner is invaluable, it cannot be permitted to inhibit the initiation and execution of essential programs as need arises.

With this in mind, let us now look at the Ontario water-management program. It is, of course, only one of many important facets of the whole urban development problem.

Our ancestors settled in an unspoiled land of seemingly unlimited resources – a land easily capable of absorbing the wastes of its human population. Nourished by these same resources, the human inhabitants have multiplied greatly and have grouped themselves into the giant urban concentrations that now characterize our two nations.

In and around these urban concentrations the vast and productive industrial and agricultural establishments upon which, in large measure, our economy is based, have developed. The advance of technology in recent years has intensified the problem with respect to both water supply and pollution control. Domestic water needs are on the increase. Indeed, the average family today uses as much water in a single day as many families used in a week a generation ago. Modern farming methods make greater and greater demands. The use of irrigation is becoming increasingly widespread.

However, by far the greatest increase in the use of water is to be found in the manufacturing segment of our economy, where huge quantities are required in industrial processes. Consider that it takes upwards of 19,000 gallons to produce a ton of steel, and as much as 65,000 gallons to turn out a ton of paper! There are relatively few industries which do not use water in quantity, and there are, therefore, equally few industries which do not have to dispose of liquid wastes.

Water is a convenient carrier of waste products and waste disposal is one of its most important uses. Aside from the factor of convenience there is nothing that approaches the enormous purifying capacity of water. But, while every stream has a degree of natural self-cleansing ability, there is a limit to the waste loads that it can assimilate. When this limit is exceeded, pollution results. It is for this reason that wastes must be properly treated before being discharged into streams. In other words, the solution of the pollution problem lies in the provision of adequate sewage treatment facilities to handle these enormous flows of domestic and industrial wastes.

It is not difficult to understand why pollution problems increase in importance as our technology and our population grow. During the past twenty years, the population of Ontario has almost doubled. From about four million at the end of World War II, it has now reached seven million, and, significantly, practically all of this expansion has taken place in urban areas.

The first and obvious requirement of a growing population is housing. The demand for housing during the postwar years outstripped the ability of municipal agencies to provide adequate new or expanded water and sewage treatment facilities. As a consequence, extensive use was made of septic tank sewage-disposal systems; existing sewage-treatment plants, too, were soon operating far beyond their design capacity. Concurrent with the waste disposal problem were the problems of water shortages and water quality in various areas of the province. Compounding the overall problem was the need to provide for industrial, educational, and commercial developments, often in areas where sufficient suitable land for the construction of adequate septic tank systems was lacking.

Closely related to the sewage-disposal problem was the large-scale use of individual wells – dug, driven, or drilled. Actual water shortages due to falling water tables were exacerbated by public health problems due in many instances to well pollution caused by the proximity of overloaded septic-tank systems or by surface run-off. It was a combination of these problems which led the federal government to discontinue its practice of lending money, through Central Mortgage and Housing Corporation under the National Housing Act, for the financing of large-scale developments unless community water supplies were available.

The reluctance of Central Mortgage and Housing Corporation to finance the construction of homes served by individual water and sewage systems resulted in many temporary, small, inadequate water and sewage works systems. In the Toronto area, for instance, some twenty-one sewage-treatment plants were operating at one time. In many cases they were discharging inadequately treated wastes into streams. In other instances, subdivision developers undertook to provide and operate water and sewage works facilities – a responsibility entirely outside their basic interests! With the overloading or breakdown of such installations, and the resulting public reaction to the pollution problems and health hazards involved, the only solution in many cases was for the municipality to take over these facilities. The problems created by residential development during these post-war years were, of course, aggravated by the rapid expansion of industry.

Such, then, were the problems facing the government of Ontario at the beginning of the 1950s. They have been presented in some detail, but you will realize that they are not peculiar to Ontario, but are common to all areas experiencing domestic and industrial expansion.

In 1956 the government of Ontario took positive action by setting up an agency to be responsible for the waters of the province, including water supply and pollution control. Under the authority of the Ontario Water Resources Commission Act of 1957, the newly formed commission undertook a comprehensive program aimed at the provision of adequate water supplies to Ontario municipalities. It was responsible also for the restoration of the water resources to acceptable standards of quality, where necessary.

It was recognized that the solution to the pollution problem lay largely in the provision of adequate treatment facilities. Emphasis was, therefore, put on the construction of such works. In the past ten years, water supply and sewage-treatment works valued at more than $1 billion have been constructed or are under active development in Ontario.

All plans for water supply or sewage-treatment works undertaken must be approved by the Ontario Water Resources Commission. Furthermore, the commission is authorized to enter into agreements with municipalities to finance, construct, and operate facilities on behalf of individual municipalities or groups of municipalities. They in turn accept the obligation of repaying the debt over a specific number of years. To date, a total of 348 water and sewerage projects has been undertaken on this basis at a cost of more than $137 million.

By 1964, owing to the acceleration throughout the province in the construction of water and sewerage works under agreement with the Ontario Water Resources Commission, most of the municipalities that could use this type of financing had new facilities in operation or under construction. Nevertheless, there were still many that could not proceed, either on the basis of their own financing or that of the commission, because of their inability to sustain further capital debt. For this reason, the authority of the Ontario Water Resources Commission was extended in 1964 to allow construction of provincially owned water projects with a service contract for the supply of its water needs signed by the municipality.

The first of these new projects was the Lake Huron Water Supply System, a 30-mile pipeline from Lake Huron to the London area, the construction of which is now nearing completion.* The cost of this pipeline, with a capacity of 67 million gallons per day, is approximately $18 million and it will serve a number of participating municipalities as well as the city of London. A similar project has been approved for St. Thomas and the surrounding area, including sections of the townships of Yarmouth and Southwold and the project is under way.* To digress, I had the pleasure on June 28, 1966, of turning the first sod for the new $65 million Ford of Canada Assembly Plant near St. Thomas. The water supply essential to the operation of this new factory will be provided by the new Lake Erie–St. Thomas pipeline, and there can be no doubt that the plant would not have been possible without the assurance of an adequate supply of suitable water.

Other pipeline proposals to serve the counties of Lambton, Peel, Kent, and the lower Grand Valley are now being studied by the commission and the municipalities within these areas.

In August 1965 we extended the provincial financing arrangement to include sewerage works on both a regional and an individual municipality basis. This means that sewage will be received and treated at provincially owned plants with charges being levied on a volume basis.

The advantages of this program are apparent. For example, no additional capital debt need be undertaken by a municipality; the province will construct oversized works to accommodate anticipated growth. This method of financing is providing further stimulus to the construction of water supply and pollution-control works in Ontario.

*Completed in 1968.

These measures will bring pollution from municipal
sources under effective control. The number of municipalities in Ontario with sanitary sewers discharging raw sewage
is diminishing yearly. Of the 997 municipalities in Ontario,
only 26 are now in this category, and 16 of them have
already presented programs for the construction of the
necessary works. In addition, many other communities that
are without sewage systems are now preparing to have
them installed.

Let us now turn to what is perhaps the most controversial
aspect of water management, industrial waste pollution.
The problems are of a somewhat different nature because
of the volume and complexity of the effluents to be treated.
Clearly, we can accept as our ultimate objective nothing
less than the complete elimination of all pollution. On the
other hand, we cannot accept the thesis that this objective
can be achieved only by immediate unilateral restriction or
closing down of established industries.

Substantial progress has already been made in this area
without major disruptions of industry and without the
necessity of imposing unwarranted or impossible financial
burdens on particular companies. The provisions of the Ontario Water Resources Commission Act are, of course, both
specific and comprehensive, and we are fully prepared to
invoke these provisions to the fullest extent should it prove
necessary for the achievement of our objectives.

Industrial water pollution is receiving the most intense
scrutiny by the commission. During 1965, it consulted with
more than 600 industries known to be discharging improperly treated wastes into surface waters. In each case, a
schedule of waste control was set out, and the absolute
necessity of achieving this objective within a reasonable
period of time was emphasized. Municipalities were ad-
vised of their responsibility for the control of waste dis-

charges to sanitary sewerage systems and urged to enact suitable by-laws for this purpose.

Furthermore, the control of industrial wastes as a requirement for all new industry was brought to the attention of industrial commissioners as a part of the commission's program to prevent further pollution. Plans for wet process industrial waste treatment facilities must be submitted to the Ontario Water Resources Commission for approval before any development is authorized, in the same way as plans for municipal treatment facilities require its approval.

The staff of the commission have held many meetings with the representatives of new industry concerning the installation of treatment facilities. Increased surveillance of pollution sources, including the use of aircraft patrols, is being undertaken. Because of technical or cost considerations, the installation of waste control facilities on a staged basis has been explored in some cases, but delay in implementing essential treatment works can not be tolerated.

Industry, it must be pointed out, has generally recognized its responsibility for pollution control and is acting accordingly. Since the Ontario Water Resources Commission was formed, industries not connected to municipal systems have spent more than $110 million on waste-treatment processes, most of it over the last few years. For example, the pulp and paper industry is engaged in a major staged program of pollution abatement, and treatment facilities in connection with the steel and oil industries costing several millions of dollars have been approved. Nevertheless, with the swiftly moving technology of today and the resulting complex industrial wastes, continually improving waste-treatment methods and constant surveillance by both industry and government are essential to the attainment and retention of effective control.

Our ultimate objective – and this can not be stressed too

strongly – is virtually complete control of industrial pollution. A very substantial proportion of this control will be achieved within the next few years.

We are also engaged in research and investigations directed towards the long-term aspects of water management. As a result of a reference from the federal governments of Canada and the United States to the International Joint Commission, Ontario is involved in a program of investigation of pollution in the Great Lakes in co-operation with the appropriate departments of the federal government. At the present time, the Ontario Water Resources Commission is working on Lake St. Clair, the Detroit River, Lake Erie, and Lake Ontario. Specifically, the commission is concentrating upon an inventory of waste-water discharges flowing directly into the lakes, an investigation of harbour pollution and of water quality in the littoral areas.

The federal Department of Mines and Technical Surveys is conducting deepwater investigations of Lake Ontario to obtain a general picture of the pollution problem. Particular attention is being given to the physical, chemical, and bacteriological qualities of the lake. The federal Department of Health and Welfare is undertaking a similar program, concentrating upon the near-shore area of the Bay of Quinte and the international section of the St. Lawrence River. In addition, the Fisheries Research Board of Canada has undertaken responsibility for a study of the productivity and enrichment of the Great Lakes and the cause and effect of nutrients entering the waters.

The continuing importance of the Great Lakes to both Canada and the United States makes it essential that we move forward in a co-ordinated effort to ensure that the quantity and quality of all the waters of all the lakes be maintained.

Any discussion of Ontario's water management program would be incomplete without a reference to our northern water resources. In the face of growing shortages in other areas, it was felt desirable that an assessment should be made of the quantity and quality of waters in the northern river basins. There has been considerable discussion about the possibility of exporting water to the United States. It is our opinion that, before any serious thought can be given to the export of water, we must have an inventory of our water resources and of our own potential future needs.

With this in mind, the government of Ontario initiated a study in 1965 of the five major northern river systems – the Severn, Winisk, Attawapiskat, Albany, and Moose. These five systems drain an area of about 173,000 square miles, about half the land area of the entire province. The study is being carried out by the Ontario Water Resources Commission with the co-operation of various departments and agencies of the provincial and federal governments.

This, then, is in brief, the story of water management in Ontario. It is only one of a complex of interrelated factors, each of which is potentially critical during this period of transition to a predominantly urban society.

An adequate quantity and quality of water is essential to the future well-being of this continent. Our water management programs must be expanded and improved, but it is essential that they be fully integrated as quickly as possible with every factor bearing on successful urban, industrial, economic, and social development.

Recognizing this, I conclude by reaffirming unequivocally Ontario's support for the whole planning process. Our attitude towards the need for comprehensive planning was set forth clearly in a white paper entitled "Design for Development," which, although it outlines our program in considerable detail, can be expressed in a single statement – a blueprint for co-ordinating the planning effort of the public and private agencies in the province of Ontario. In accordance with the provisions of the white paper, we have already established a cabinet committee on regional development, which bears the responsibility for leadership in this important undertaking. Perhaps the most important component of the program is its clear recognition of the need to include in a direct and meaningful manner the citizens, principally through regional development councils, and the universities through utilization of their research capability.

There can be no doubt that this powerful focus of action and research will enable us to deal swiftly and effectively, both now and in the years ahead, with the many new problems stemming from Ontario's burgeoning population and prosperity.

4. ECONOMIC AND BUSINESS IMPLICATIONS

How Business Lives with the Border

G. R. HEFFERNAN

IN VIEWING THE BORDER between Canada and the United States, there are two basic positions taken by businessmen. One group sees it as a barrier to the expansion of trade, as a hurdle, the crossing of which requires a major effort, and as the source of irritating bureaucratic regulations that impede the normal and logical transaction of business. The members of the other group see the border as a protective umbrella absolutely essential to their business survival and view any attempt at lowering the barrier with fear and suspicion that sometimes reach irrational proportions. Elements of the two groups are found on each side of the border, with a stronghold of "protectionism" apparent in highly industrialized Southern Ontario.

If the developing megalopolis is considered without the complication of the border, one cannot fail to see a highly integrated system of interdependent industries which, because of its concentration, sophistication, and large market, should form a trading area competitive with any other in the world. At the same time, it is apparent that two other major, highly integrated industrial complexes are in an advanced stage of development, one in Western Europe and one in Japan. These two large and efficient trading complexes are now competing very successfully in our international megalopolitan area with a long list of industrial and consumer products.

This competition poses a threat and a challenge to industry within the international megalopolis – a threat that the protectionist would meet with higher tariffs and the free trader with the rationalization of industry across the megalopolitan border to produce products at lower cost. With the present trend towards economic internationalism as opposed to the narrow economic nationalism that became a major force in the late nineteenth century, it would seem that the free trader is more in tune with the times than the protectionist. The success of the Common Market in Europe has provided a lesson that should not be ignored by businessmen of the international megalopolis. A step in the direction of freer trade within the megalopolitan area has been made in the Canadian–US automotive agreement, which provides for the free movement of automobiles and automotive parts across the border. The manufacturer is free to decide where he can most advantageously make his units and parts, with a view to specializing production and improving the overall imbalance in the automotive trade between the US and Canada. This type of rationalization means that costs can be reduced through optimum production runs and, as a result, competition from other sources can be more successfully met. The principle, if applied on a broader scale, could lead to US–Canadian free trade in other industries which would be of particular benefit to the megalopolitan area. It is not my intention to attempt to outline in detail just how this area should be developed; this is a job for experts with full command of the statistical and technical information required to make plans for an orderly transition. The automotive agreement was unique in that the industry is comprised of a few large companies operating on both sides of the border. It was possible as a result of this close control to overcome many of the obstacles that would occur in a more widespread industry with independent companies operating in each country.

Free trade between the two countries is not a new idea. There is now free flow of about 50 per cent of our trade across the border, mainly in the form of raw materials.

There can be little doubt that this free flow has been beneficial to the economies of both countries. A good example is provided by the steel industry, in which we see Canadian ore meeting us coal in Chicago, Detroit, Cleveland, Buffalo, and Hamilton. Steel scrap also flows freely, moving from surplus to deficit areas regardless of the border. A lifting of the tariff barriers on finished products would lead to a corresponding increase in the efficiency of the steel industry within the megalopolis and a greater ability to meet other foreign competition.

One of the results of the rationalization of industry between the two countries would be a greater degree of economic dependence and a lower degree of national self-sufficiency. Of course, the protectionists beat the drum of national security. However, it appears obvious that our economies are irrevocably interlocked and that the defence of North America has become a matter for joint action. In the context of North American continental defence a policy of national self-sufficiency no longer has validity, while national tariff barriers within a continent in a world moving toward freer trade are an anachronism.

There will be alarm from those who see in the growth of the megalopolis a prime target area for nuclear bombs. But that is another problem. The megalopolis is here and is going to continue its growth regardless of what we do. Our problem is to make it as livable as possible and to gain the maximum in economic advantage from it, not merely suffer its inconveniences. There are strong arguments for regional industrial development from both a humanitarian and a strategic point of view. This, however, has nothing to do with the border, or with how the businessman sees the border. Regional development will go on in North America on both sides of the border with or without tariffs and, although influenced by tariff structures, it will not be dependent upon them.

The movement towards wage parity, which is being successfully advocated by such major international unions as the Automotive Workers and the United Steelworkers of America, poses a problem for the Canadian businessman. Because he is faced with paying the same wages as his US counterpart, he must increase his productivity per man-hour to meet US as well as other foreign competition. The fact that this increase in productivity can best be achieved through the degree of automation made possible by long production runs should give urgency in Canada to the development of a free or freer trade area.

The move towards freer trade should not involve an abrupt removal of tariffs, since this could cause serious dislocation of industry in both countries. A joint US–Canadian study on an industry-by-industry basis should be carried out as a preliminary step towards establishing an orderly withdrawal of tariffs. The steel industry might well be a logical place to start, since the US and Canadian industries are already interdependent in the field of major raw materials. The pulp and paper, chemical, petroleum, electrical, metallurgical, and appliance industries also lend themselves to such studies.

Another obstacle to trade which is hindering the efficient development of commerce within the megalopolitan area is of a negative rather than a positive nature and involves the lack of truly efficient transportation across the border.

The Seaway has had a far reaching and beneficial effect in opening points on the Great Lakes to two-way intercontinental trade. It has not, however, had any appreciable effect on transportation across the border. We are still hampered by the tedious and frustrating business of trying to resolve rail rates between the US and Canadian railroads. Lack of co-ordination between the states and provinces on such things as highway load limits and highway regulations is a major stumbling block. The most serious problem is manifest in our failure to utilize the potential for cheap water transportation within the megalopolis provided by the Great Lakes system. While bulk commodities are moving efficiently on the Lakes, cheap barge transportation on shipments ranging from 500 to 1,000 tons per barge does not exist. The border itself is not the basic problem, but rather the lack of low-cost handling at terminal points and a gap in the technology of barge movement on the Lakes. The seasonal aspect of water movement, which again is a technological matter, merits consideration by international experts. I am not going to attempt to provide solutions, but merely point out that it is sometimes cheaper to ship goods from Europe to Chicago than it is to ship the same goods from Toronto to Chicago.

To sum up the question of "How Business Lives with the Border," it is apparent that we are not taking full advantage of our participation in the world's greatest industrial complex and the world's greatest market. This advantage is being offset to a large extent by tariffs across the border and a lack of efficient transportation within the complex. The Great Lakes megalopolitan trading area is under heavy pressure from foreign imports, particularly those from Western Europe and Japan. This pressure is continuing to build up in an ever-widening range of products, and it can best be met by a lowering of tariff barriers and an improvement in transportation, both of which will tend to lower production costs within the megalopolis.

How Business Lives with the Border

RONALD S. RITCHIE

THE BORDER BETWEEN Canada and the United States naturally brings to mind factors that rather arbitrarily divide our two countries, even in areas where natural forces would appear to suggest integration. Many of the most obvious examples are in the economic sector. Immigration and entry laws impede the mobility of labour. Tariffs and currency differences inhibit the flow of goods from points of most economic production to their natural markets. Despite such obstacles, an impressive degree of economic integration has occurred across the border, a fact to which the international megalopolis theme of this seminar bears witness. More is in prospect, and it is possible that in the future that part of the international megalopolis lying to the north of Lakes Erie and Ontario will be even more closely linked to the megalopolis which Dr. Doxiadis identifies as stretching from Chicago south of the Great Lakes to the Atlantic seaboard.

Let us turn our attention to an area in which the fact of the border must lead us more and more into new and effective forms of co-operation and co-ordination. I propose to speak of two great resources which we have no choice but to share, partly because they lie across the border, and partly because, by their very nature, they cannot be confined by it. These are, of course, air and water. The common description of the subject is pollution control. Many of us could agree that the quality of the management of our air and our water may well be a critical determinant of the life cycle of the megalopolis. We could probably also agree that, whether it is a question of failure to manage these resources or a question of the choices to be made for their satisfactory management, business is directly involved.

Examples of the management problems shared by our two countries are easy to cite. Together we have helped to make Lake Erie into what has sometimes been called "the largest cesspool in the world." Not the least of the costs of having done so is the present state of the commercial fishing operations formerly carried on there by both countries.

Only a few years ago Ontario tobacco crops to the north

of Lake Erie suffered some $5,000,000 worth of damage from atmospheric ozone, the product of photochemical reactions among oxides and unsaturated hydrocarbons discharged into the air by the industrial complexes south of the lake. It is a normal phenomenon, when high- and low-pressure areas are in the required relative relationship, for Sarnia's chemical valley too finds itself ventilated from the Chicago area. At such times a startling increase in oxidants is recorded, an indication that Sarnia is feeling the results of photochemical activity on substances injected into the atmosphere by the huge industrial and urban complex located around the southern end of Lake Michigan.

Of the two resources shared across the border, water is probably the easier to manage. In the area adjacent to, and divided between, the two national sectors of the international megalopolis, we jointly possess the largest inland fresh waterway system in the world. Lake Erie is evidence of past carelessness, lack of co-ordination, and lack of agreed standards of control. Arriving at these agreed standards of control is complicated by the number and variety of municipalities and individual industrial enterprises involved. In general, however, the technology to deal with the physical aspects of the problem is available, even though the direct costs incurred will often be high for municipalities and industry alike.

The basic need here, then, is for an agreed assessment and jointly accepted standards. In concept, the problem of the use of an international river for waste disposal by the immediately adjoining sections of the megalopolis can be resolved by fairly simple means on the basis of the quality of the incoming water and the desired quality of the discharge from the river. The calculated capacity can then be shared equally between the two countries and apportioned to individual sources by provincial and state control agencies.

The problem of the Great Lakes megalopolis is somewhat more complicated because the whole drainage basin must be controlled as a unit. The Great Lakes drainage basin involves a land area of some 200,000 square miles and a water area of 100,000 square miles with an average discharge to the St. Lawrence River of some 280,000 cubic feet per second. There can be no doubt that it is and will be a very complex task to operate such an area as a utility to meet the requirements of drinking water, recreation, commercial fishing, transportation, and waste disposal. Complex as the task must be, recent studies of the Delaware River Basin and its far from simple estuary show that the problems of such a system can be effectively sorted out by the computer technology now available.

Given such an assessment and the resulting agreed standards of control, and given further the assurance that no municipality or business will nullify standards that others are required to maintain, there can be no doubt that the problem of the management of our jointly shared water resource is soluble at its present stage. We should, however, ask ourselves what the burden of waste disposal on the Great Lakes system forty years from now will be. Certainly, the hugely expanded population and industrial activity which can be foreseen for our international megalopolis will increase the burden likely to be thrown on the Great Lakes waterway system by that time. Estimates should be made now, comparing the likely level with allowable effluent standards, while there is still time to plan for a new technology of waste disposal, or perhaps even for regulation of the location of populations and industries.

Management of our mutually shared resource poses much more serious problems conceptually, technologically, and probably even in terms of the forms of consultation, cooperation, and control required. Air pollution may well prove to be a much more critical factor in the long-run prospects of megalopolis than water pollution. Its effects are much less predictable, at least at present, and are apt to be spread over a much larger geographic and much less manageable area than that required for detailed considera-tion of the water control of the Great Lakes system. For in-stance, what is sometimes called in Canada the "Grey Cup inversion of 1962" was actually part of a massive stagnation covering the area from the Great Lakes to Georgia and from Arkansas to the Atlantic. Some 87 million people were exposed to high concentrations of pollution which accumu-lated in the stagnant air mass for from five to seven days.

Our understanding of the causes of air pollution and our available technology for controlling it are inadequate for the needs of today, let alone the threats of the future. Despite a massive effort on a number of fronts to find and apply cures, Los Angeles is still far from solving its smog problem. It might be noted that Los Angeles has a much more localized problem than does our international megalopolis.

Not all of the problems of air pollutants are so difficult. An important group is composed largely of neighbourhood nuisances created by particulate matter — sulphur oxides, halogens, carbon monoxide, hydrogen sulphides, and odours which can be made innocuous by available pro-cesses within the plant or can be removed or dispersed through properly designed stacks. Even neighbourhood nuisances can have their cross-border implications as Port Huron, Michigan, and Windsor, Ontario, can testify from time to time. Nor can it be assumed that their control is necessarily cheap, since it may require very expensive pro-cesses or even the provision of buffer areas between resi-dential and heavy industry zones.

It is in the area of photochemical smogs that we appear to still have most to learn. They are produced by reactions in the atmosphere between nitrogen oxides, sulphur oxides, and unsaturated hydrocarbons. Their control in our indus-trialized and mechanized society is not effective with present technology. The sources are diverse and the chemical activity involved may be widespread. Local weather conditions usually play the major role in their distribution and can be used in planning the necessary corrective measures. Occasionally, however, massive weather systems override local conditions with unfortunate results which may be spectacular in sweep and intensity. Before we can come to any agreement on detailed effective control of the many and varied activities involved, and perhaps before we can even begin to decide on the geographic boundaries within which controls must be co-operatively established, there is much to be learned.

It is evident that business and industry have an important and continuing role to play in these critical tasks of effective management of our air and water resources within the Great Lakes megalopolis area. Their role needs, however, to be seen in perspective. The overall task of assessment, co-ordination, and agreement on control standards is not the task of industry, although its fund of information, its research resources, and its participation may well be required in this task. The proper balance to be sought between maximum permitted standards of pollution, on the one hand, and the real costs to society of achieving them, on the other, is not its decision, although information and advice from businessmen are essential in the search for this balance.

The recognition that we are dealing here with social costs and social benefits, and with a balance between them, is of fundamental importance. To a significant degree, standards of control lack value except to the extent that they are part of a pattern designed to meet overall agreed objectives. In a very real way, too, the application of standards by an individual firm, or even a municipality, may be wasteful unless there is assurance that other firms or other municipalities are conforming to co-ordinated standards in the interests of an agreed objective. So far as the role of business is concerned, there is little or no question of a choice between pollution and profit. Control of pollution requires capital and involves expense, often on a large scale. These costs can be borne and this capital provided only through the prices of goods and services and the taxes imposed by governments, or a combination of the two. Business has a role, but only that of one among many participants in the task of air and water resource management. The total task is on a scale appropriate to the scale of the international megalopolis itself, whose future may well depend on how that task is handled.

An Economist Looks at the Future International Megalopolis

ANTHONY DOWNS

THE TERM "INTERNATIONAL MEGALOPOLIS" has an exciting and even glamorous ring. So do the sweeping panoramas set forth by some of the other contributors to this volume, who forecast a vast belt of urbanized areas linking two nations in the Great Lakes region. But as a practising, and therefore practical, economist, I must assess this intriguing concept in the hard light of reality. My assessment consists of three main parts. The first is a discussion of how fast the so-called megalopolis will actually appear, and how international its effects will actually be. The second is an examination of several major implications of the forces causing "megalopolitan" developments in our society. The third is a brief summary of conclusions.

1 FUTURE METROPOLITAN GROWTH – MEGALOPOLITAN OR
INTERNATIONAL?

Although my colleagues foresee an "international megalopolis" in the Great Lakes region, I should like to point out
three important qualifications:

A *How Fast Will the Great Lakes Region Become
Megalopolitan?*
First, I do not believe that the kind of continuous urbanized
development implied by the term "megalopolis" will really
materialize in this region for a long time. An enormous
amount of open space still separates even those large cities
which are relatively close together, and this space can hold
very large populations even at low density. For example,
Chicago and Milwaukee are considered close neighbours,
but they are actually about 75 miles apart. Although developed areas stretch south from Milwaukee for many
miles, and north from Chicago for many more, it would be
fair to say that an undeveloped belt of land at least 45 miles
long and 10 miles wide still lies between them. This belt
would be quite suitable for residential and other development. If residences actually occupied only 50 per cent of it,
they would cover 225 square miles, or 144,000 acres. At
four families per acre (a very low density) and 3.2 persons
per family (low for outlying areas), this one belt alone
would hold a future population of 1.8 million persons.
In comparison, the population of the entire Chicago metropolitan area grew by only 1.04 million persons from 1950 to
1960. And this growth was based upon unusually high immigration and birth rates, and included expansion in all
directions.

Thus it might take as long as three or four decades for
the area between these two neighbouring cities to become
"solidly" built up, even at low suburban densities. It will
take longer for similar development to link up other major
cities, because they are much farther apart. The horizon for

the arrival of "megalopolitan society" in the Great Lakes region in terms of spatial settlement patterns, I am forced to conclude, is a very distant one – probably at least fifty years.

B *The Uncertainty of Long-Range Forecasting*
It seems that a really continuously built-up megalopolis will not arrive for such a long time that unforeseeable changes in other major factors might render any forecasts we make today highly inaccurate. Long-range prophecies are extremely hazardous in an era of superspeed technical change. Think back fifty years and try to forecast what is happening today. Would you have anticipated suburban sprawl, Negro ghettos, smog, jet travel?

Even now, we can see some technically feasible developments which might alter the spatial pattern of cities. Cheap TV-telephones accompanied by cheap document copiers operating on telephone lines – and guaranteed free from wire-tapping – might radically reduce the need for any downtown concentration of leading officials. High-speed automated highways or rail lines might further disperse cities. Other developments such as supersonic transports, huge airliners carrying nearly 1,000 passengers, and vastly improved educational TV will also effect great changes in our style of living. Consequently, it is dangerously speculative to project existing trends 50 years into the future and conclude that we will have a megalopolis around the Great Lakes.

C *How International Would a Great Lakes Megalopolis Be?*
If and when the Great Lakes region does become truly megalopolitan, the international implications of this development will probably not be as significant as the purely national ones. There are three main reasons why urban growth could spill over the international boundaries at specific points. First, international commercial activity might expand at border-crossing points because of growth

in tourism and trade. This would attract firms and government agencies in both countries specializing in these activities to border cities. However, improvements in transportation are likely to weaken this effect in the future, even if tourism and trade do continue to grow. Tourists will be able to drive rapidly past border-crossing points unless there is some particular attraction such as Niagara Falls. Or they will fly directly to interior points and overpass the border. The same is true of commercial activity.

The second possible cause of international urban spillover is the clustering of workers on one side of the border, with the firms that employ them on the other. This is practical on the US-Mexican border because of the very low wage structure in Mexico. But it is not nearly as significant on the Canadian-US border because wage differentials are small. In fact, the likelihood of such spill-over depends more upon the economic policies of the two nations than upon the form of future urban settlement, as we shall see.

A third possible source of border conglomeration would be the construction of housing or other developments on one side because it brings them closer to the central business district of a major city on the other side than its own suburbs. This might be the case in Windsor, for example, since the borders of its built-up areas are much closer to downtown Detroit than the suburban fringes of that city. Yet nationality imposes a severe barrier to such a development. Residents of Detroit do not regard a choice of houses in Windsor vs. Grosse Point as simply a housing decision. It is also a nationality decision, and most citizens on both sides are reluctant to shift countries just for commuting convenience. Furthermore, future changes will make this a diminishing force, because the relative pull of central business districts will decline. New growth is dispersing industrial, office, retail, commercial, and all other facilities more widely in each sprawling metropolitan area. Hence the advantage of proximity to downtown is declining, and will decline more.

In fact, the international aspects of future megalopolitan development in this area will be much more heavily influenced by other types of policies than by purely spatial settlement patterns. For example, if the US maintains a tight labour market for many years while Canada does not, then the US need for workers may attract rural Canadians into urban complexes opposite US cities. But if Canada's labour market is just as tight, then Canadian workers will stay in their own cities. So the relative labour force conditions in both nations are more crucial than the spatial forms of these cities.

Other key factors influencing the amount of international intercourse in the megalopolis are the degree and extent of nationalistic feelings – especially in Canada – and how these feelings are reflected in economic policies. The more US investment in Canada is encouraged, the more international activity will occur. Future communications developments, particularly the linking of nations together via satellites in worldwide TV networks, may weaken disruptive nationalistic feelings, but no prediction can be made with any assurance.

Finally, sprawling spatial growth will tend to locate people on both sides of the border farther from the crossing points where the international aspects are now concentrated. Thus the more megalopolitan we become, the less international we may be, in terms of spatial settlement.

2 FORCES TENDING TOWARDS MEGALOPOLITAN DEVELOPMENT

The economic implications of future urban growth forms cannot be readily separated from several other implications. These have traditionally been labelled social, cultural, political, and educational, but I regard them as inseparable from economic. Therefore, my discussion of the key implications of those forces tending to shape a megalopolitan society will contain elements of all these aspects of what we might simply call urban living in the future.

A Increasing Range of Individual Choice

Today almost everyone laments living in an increasingly bureaucratized society. Many even look back nostalgically towards earlier days free from red tape and regulations. But any really honest appraisal of North American society reveals an astonishing increase in the range of choices open to most individuals. In spite of the regulations we sometimes endure, the average middle-class citizen of North America has a freedom of action unprecedented in human history. He can jet anywhere in the world within 48 hours, and pay for the trip later. He can turn on his colour TV and get a front-row seat at a football game being played 2,000 miles away. He can listen to his choice of symphony in stereo by putting on a record, drive to a nearby shopping centre with a dazzling array of things to buy, or go for a ride in the country in his air-conditioned, stereo-sound-filled, automatically shifted car. In short, he lives in a world with constantly expanding, almost exploding, options available for his use, and he can actually afford to take advantage of an ever increasing number of those options.

The major reasons for this remarkable expansion of choice are well-known, so I shall mention them only briefly:

1

Rising standards of living mean that people need to devote less of their incomes to necessities and can spend more in discretionary ways suited to their individual tastes and desires.

2

Greater leisure time means that their role in life makes them consumers rather than producers.

3

Faster and less expensive transportation has not only opened up whole areas of the world to people who could never reach them before, but has also restructured the metropolitan areas in which we live.

4

Greater educational levels are achieved not only through more formal education, but also through constant exposure to a bewildering variety of stimuli from TV, newspapers, movies, magazines, etc. Just being a consumer today is an extremely complex activity requiring a very sophisticated education in both the creation and the satisfaction of tastes.

5

Rapid technical change and increased social specialization continuously enlarge the number of activities from which we can choose. Even in such a mundane field as real estate, the development of condominium arrangements and associations of homeowners has expanded the range of types of ownership available to families. They can now buy a share in a swimming pool, a beach, and a riding stable when they buy a home.

In the absence of any great war or other social upheaval, it seems that all these choice-expanding forces will continue to operate during the next few decades. Hence the freedom of action of the average individual on both sides of the border will become ever greater.

What will be the major implications of such an expansion of choice in terms of the future megalopolis? These are my predictions:

1

Urban development will continue to sprawl across the landscape, rather than shift to higher concentration. In spite of the anguished protests of many city planners and of central-city mayors, most North Americans like the so-called urban sprawl, or "slurbs." Since the most likely technical developments in communication and transportation will tend to increase personal mobility, most people will work in scattered work places, and live at greater distances from their work. At least I foresee no major tendency to reverse the historically continuous dispersal of population across the landscape. True, people with tastes for more urban living will cluster in large central cities. Moreover, nodes of higher density development will appear around regional shopping centres, office centres, and universities. Nevertheless, I do not foresee the deliberate construction of any really high-density communities in the future. Even though the densities of existing central cities may rise, the bulk of population expansion will undoubtedly occur in suburb-like developments. Thus the entire concept of the megalopolis of the future becomes credible.

2

Society will experience a greater heterogeneity of living styles. In the past, it was quite possible to tell a great deal about a man by knowing any one of several things concerning him. For example, if you merely knew his income, you could probably make an accurate estimate of the kind of house he lived in, his educational level, the type of occupation he had, his political party, and many of his tastes. But the tremendous expansion of individual choices is gradually eroding such "clusters of characteristics." In the future, we shall see more and more heterogeneity in all aspects of human life. Knowing that a man has a certain income, or has attained a certain educational level, will tell us less and less about his other characteristics, because of the tremendous variety of choices open to him, and his greater inclination to exercise individual discretion in making those choices. This heterogeneity will reflect itself in an increased diversity of styles of living within the megalopolis. Thus, there will be high-rise buildings in the suburbs and on lakes, low-density developments in central cities, developments peopled entirely by older folks, and others peopled only by young "swingers," mixed developments – in short, almost every conceivable combination.

3

There will be a decreasing attachment of individuals to specific neighbourhoods or communities. This tendency is so important that it will be discussed separately.

In general, a person's freedom of choice will be directly dependent upon his income, except among certain ethnic minorities. This will not only reflect the fact that money will continue to open many doors of opportunity, but also the fact that those people who have ability and education will be able to earn high incomes.

B *Possible Development of Greater Social Divergence and Tensions*

Unfortunately, while choice expands for the majority of North Americans, a significant group may be left behind – the deprived minority of the North American population. This group consists of the lowest income segments of the United States and Canada, and also – particularly in the United States – of ethnic and national minorities. In the past, their opportunities have expanded far less rapidly than those of the average citizen in society. Blocked from participation in the fruits of technical change by low incomes, ethnic discrimination, and lack of education, they have failed to increase their welfare at the same extraordinary rate as the people discussed above. It is true, however, that even the lowest income groups in the United States and Canada have experienced significant increases in absolute living standards during the past two decades. Moreover, by the standards of poverty elsewhere in the world, they are almost rich. Nevertheless, our society cannot long stand striking disparities in living standards among its major elements without severe conflict and tension.

This inability to sustain strong divergences in standards of living among major groups is a new factor in our society. In all past history a small and extremely wealthy upper class co-existed in relative peace with a large and extremely poor lower class. This still occurs in much of the world today, but I do not believe, for two reasons, that it is any longer possible in North America. First, it contradicts the basic ethos of our society. Our vociferous advocacy of democracy, prosperity, and equality of opportunity creates revolutionary aspirations among those who find themselves unable to achieve these ideal conditions.

Second, the communications industry in our society constantly exposes the lowest income groups to images bound to stimulate their dissatisfaction. These images show intimate views of others with much higher standards of living, and offer continuous demonstrations that social protests launched by tiny but loud groups are likely to be effective. It was not television that created the civil rights movement in the United States, but television made it effective and continues to sustain it. Similarly, television is also creating and sustaining the "white backlash" which so alarms many of us. And television is here to stay.

If the middle income and upper income groups in our society continue to get wealthier, while the lower income groups – particularly racial minorities – find themselves more and more disadvantaged, we can expect trouble and violence. This will occur even if the lower income groups experience absolute increases in their standards of living. It is the relative disadvantage they perceive through television and other media which will motivate them to act. In this respect North America is a microcosm of the entire world. The rich nations are getting richer at a fantastic rate in relation to previous centuries, while the poor nations barely hold their own. The tension between these two divergent groups has only begun to make itself evident. When television and other worldwide communication media impress upon the deprived people just how deprived they are, we can expect far more conflict in the world. And that is the situation in our urban societies as well.

There is a real possibility that many central cities in North America, particularly in the Great Lakes and North-eastern regions of the United States, will become islands of poverty – mostly black poverty – in a sea of prosperity. In my opinion, this is the single most important domestic problem facing the United States. It has crucial implications for the future of any Great Lakes megalopolis. For example, we must develop some form of financial assistance to central city governments to prevent them from going bankrupt, since they must cope with a heavy concentration of the lowest income groups within their boundaries. Furthermore, we must ultimately disperse members of racial minorities throughout the megalopolis to prevent a geographic division of society along racial lines.

The future megalopolis will not be free from tension and conflict, even though most of its citizens may be remote from any direct physical experience with low income residents. This tension and conflict is likely to be particularly acute in a number of cities, such as Chicago, Detroit, Cleveland, Gary, Milwaukee, and Buffalo, in the Great Lakes region.

c *Decline of Place Loyalties*

One of the most significant effects of the forces of change in our society is a continuous decline in individual loyalty to any particular neighbourhood, town, city, or even region. The old feeling of belonging to a specific neighbourhood or community, and the maintenance of lifelong attachments

there are rapidly being eroded by three major developments: increasing personal mobility, greater integration of
people into a single communications system dominated by
a national viewpoint, and the declining power of local
governments.

The transportation changes which are causing an enormous increase in the physical mobility of the average individual have already been mentioned. It seems likely that
these forces will continue to accelerate. Statistics for the
entire US population show that each year about 20 per cent
of all the people in the country move from one residence to
another. Thus, in the average neighbourhood there is a
complete turnover every five years. Of course, some residents remain in the same place for decades whereas others
move two or three times a year, but the statistical average
indicates a high degree of mobility compared with most
previous societies. This annual residential turnover is even
greater in apartment areas (where it averages 30 per cent)
and in certain parts of the country, such as southern Cali-
fornia (32 per cent). Although post-war statistics show
that residential mobility has remained about the same for
twenty years, it is undoubtedly higher than before World
War II.

Another type of mobility which is increasing rapidly is
that of easy movement within each metropolitan area. The
increased use of automobiles in both the United States and
Canada – and now in Western Europe and other parts of
the world as well – and improved highways have given most
people more freedom of movement except during rush
hours. The great advantages of the privately owned automobile are its constant availability and individual flexibility
in serving the owner. It goes from exactly where he is to
exactly where he wants to be at exactly the time he wants
to go. It follows that, as the automobile becomes increas-

ingly available, the individual's attachment to a particular small area of real estate declines.

Moving from one city to another has also been made much easier by recent transportation changes. In the US, the Interstate Highway system has significantly reduced automobile travel times between major cities. Equally important, it has reduced the nervous tension inherent in driving long distances, thereby tremendously improving the quality of automobile travel. But the really great impact upon speed of movement between cities has been made by jet aircraft. The total number of airline trips has expanded rapidly since jets came into widespread use, and will probably increase even more when the giant jets such as the Boeing 747 come into use. Before World War II, a trip from Chicago to Los Angeles took forty-eight hours by train. After the war, piston airplanes cut the trip to five or six hours. Then jets cut it to three and one-half hours. In the future, if supersonic transport is used on this run, flight time will be reduced to about one hour. The resulting increase in the individual's capacity to move around this continent and the world is stunning.

Improvements in communication have also resulted in a form of "mental mobility." The telephone multiplied the psychological mobility of every individual to almost astronomical proportions, since he could actually visit a nearly infinite number of locations without leaving his desk. This feeling of mobility will be increased by TV telephones and transmission of documents and computer information over telephone lines to remote reproduction stations. The only countertrend is our recent slowdown in the speed of the US mail!

The second major factor reducing individual loyalty to specific localities is the impact of nationally oriented communications media upon individual tastes, feelings, and values. The average citizen is exposed to more nationally oriented media than ever before, mainly because of the many hours he spends viewing network TV programs. Magazines are produced for national audiences, as are books and the records on radio. Only newspapers, some local TV and radio shows, and personal conversations (still the most significant form of communication) are locally oriented.

The third loyalty-eroding factor is the declining power of local governments. This decline results from the fact that the economic realities of metropolitan life transcend local political boundaries, but local taxing and policy-making powers do not. Hence local governments are incapable of dealing with many of the major forces that shape the lives of their residents. For example, individual suburbs have difficulty influencing the routes of major expressways. And central-city governments cannot tax the wealth of the suburban residents who work in their boundaries and use their amenities to help pay for those amenities and for the welfare costs created by the low income people who live in the central cities. Therefore, the citizens of these localities, as well as local governments themselves, must increasingly look to larger political entities – especially the national governments – for help in solving their problems. This, I believe, will be even more true of the sprawling future megalopolis than it is of today's metropolis.

The universal decline in local loyalties resulting from these factors has already had, and will continue to have, profound impacts upon the nature of our society. Among the most important of these impacts are the following:

1

People are adopting an increasingly irresponsible and even hostile attitude towards their local governments. In the not so distant past, many people grew up and lived their lives within the confines of a particular neighbourhood. They naturally developed a deep interest in what went on there. Today even those persons who spend their entire lives within a single metropolitan area tend to move to different locations in that area. As they grow up, they leave home and move into the "young swingers" colony downtown. Then they marry and move again. When their children are old enough to go to school, they become "child-oriented marrieds" with a tendency to move to the suburbs. As their children grow up and leave home, they become "dynamic elders" and move to smaller quarters. Finally, when they retire from active work, they may move again.

Furthermore, as more and more firms develop national organizations, they shift their personnel around from one part of North America to another. This continual uprooting creates a greatly diminished loyalty to and concern with local governments. Hence it undermines the sense of responsibility which citizens theoretically should feel towards their local government. That government becomes an alien force to be endured, or resisted, rather than an extension of one's own powers. Since each family must deal with a number of different local governments over the span of its life, it may even come to regard each of them as an enemy rather than an instrument. Certainly this attitude is one of the many factors in our society undermining the general allegiance to law and order. The anti-government attitude it engenders has, in part, encouraged the anarchic rioting experienced in many large cities in the past few years.

In fact, this attitude of hostility towards local government probably helped elect Mayor Lindsay of New York. Just as the ancient Caesars championed the cause of the common people against the nobles, so Mayor Lindsay champions the cause of the common people against the city bureaucrats whom the people themselves support. He is an exciting knight in shining armour prepared to battle with the legally constituted but faceless governmental and private machinery which has almost paralyzed New York.

Thus I expect that this diminished allegiance of individuals to local government will create serious problems for parts of the megalopolis.

2

National governments are performing more direct and more powerful roles in local affairs. The reasons for this well-known development were described previously. Essentially, it is a form of what I modestly call "Downs's Power-Shift Law": uncontrolled conflict shifts power upward. In a bureaucracy, if two subordinates of a given official cannot agree on a particular policy, then the power over that policy shifts upward to the official himself. Similarly, in our metropolitan areas, when local governments cannot agree on how to co-ordinate their affairs, power over those affairs tends to shift upward to the state or national government. In the long run, this will weaken the political power of central cities, since the proportionate power of suburban areas in national politics is constantly growing, owing to the expansion of suburban population. Again, I believe that foreseeable trends will increase these tendencies in the future.

3

The basis of our culture in North America is gradually changing from local or even regional to national, as already reflected in the structure of social contacts maintained by the leaders in our societies. Many of the most important and influential citizens in both our countries have moved around a great deal while climbing the ladder of success. As a result, their friends and contacts are scattered throughout the country. Moreover, they know that their own activities are greatly influenced by decisions made in many locations. Therefore, they are interested in learning about and influencing behaviour in all parts of the country. Finally, improvements in transportation and communications make it possible for them to travel frequently both physically and mentally, thereby maintaining greater familiarity with more places than was ever before possible in human history.

It is undoubtedly true that this national orientation is limited to a relatively small minority in both countries. Most people still spend most of their time in a single metropolitan area, although they may live portions of their lives in several such areas. And yet the tone of society emanating from national TV networks, national magazines, national coverage by wire services, and national government decisions is much more strongly influenced by this small minority of leaders than we would perhaps like to admit. Since this leadership minority has already substantially shifted its allegiance to a national basis, and will do so even more in the future, we can expect greater cultural, as well as economic, orientation towards nationwide, and perhaps even worldwide, horizons.

D *Summary*

The analysis I have presented may seem rather strange, since it has barely mentioned the kinds of factors usually discussed by economists. But in our society economic affairs are affected to a very great extent by international, political, cultural, and social forces. In fact, as our standard of living rises, the "problem frontier" of our society will shift away from economic matters and focus on these other aspects of society.

What are the major implications of my analysis regarding the future international megalopolis in the Great Lakes region? I would summarize them as follows:

1

Metropolitan areas will spread out spatially as fast or faster than they have in the past in proportion to population growth, which will slow down.

2

It will take many decades for the Great Lakes region to

become a single continuous network of settled communities, i.e., a true megalopolis.

3

The impact of this form of urban growth upon international relations between the US and Canada will not be nearly as significant as the impact of other policies.

4

In both countries there will be decreasing loyalty among individuals towards the governments controlling their local affairs. In fact, there may be positive hostility between many citizens and their local governments, especially in neighbourhoods suffering from significant deprivations.

5

There is a significant danger that the middle income and upper income groups, especially among whites, will improve their standards of living much faster than the lowest income groups. Because of the interaction of these groups through communications media and political structures, this might generate increasingly rebellious attitudes among the lowest income groups, particularly among Negroes. The resulting violence and counterviolence may lead to more and more anarchy in our older central cities.

6

National governments will continuously expand the roles they play in local affairs, particularly in large central cities.

7

Individual choice and opportunity for middle income and upper income groups will expand at unprecedented speed, assuming they are not overly restricted by the conflicts mentioned above.

8

Personal mobility will continue to rise; more people will travel to and be familiar with more distant places than ever before.

9

A nationally oriented or even partly internationally oriented culture will gradually erode many of the local and regional elements that are still significant in the lives of most people.

All of these conclusions stem from an anticipated acceleration of the present fantastic rate of social, technical, and economic change. The price for this dizzying pace is a general loss of stability in all aspects of our lives. Yet never has the future seemed more exciting to those willing to grapple with its challenges.

Comments

E. A. G. ROBINSON

DR. DOWNS'S DEBUNKING of the distant look into the future saddened me a little. Of course he is right; we cannot foresee the year 2000, which is Dr. Doxiadis' date. The further one tries to look ahead, the more difficult it is, but I believe we should consider it a duty to attempt a forecast. It must be remembered that day by day, on the basis of very inadequate evidence, we are constructing the framework for the people of the future; we are making the world in which they will have to live. A third of the houses in which the population of 2000 will be living and conducting their complicated lives are already built. Within the next ten years more than half of the physical framework will be completed. The uncertainties of the future add to the responsibilities of those who are planning the cities and conditions for life in 2000. The more difficult it is to look ahead, the more important it is that we should be as accurate and scientific as possible.

Let me remind you that Dr. Doxiadis emphasized in his paper that he is creating a framework of thought, a system of information and of data which will help us to look ahead, but that the outcome of all this can be no better than the assumptions and the criteria put into the thinking. Our function is to try to see whether the assumptions reflect the things people will want. Why do we have city centres at all in a world in which retail trade comes nearer and nearer to the consumer and away from the city centre? In view of Dr. Downs's projections, is the need to go to the city centre for interviews or to meet people going to be as great as in the past? It is doubtful whether the need to meet people,

to talk to them face to face is going to disappear quite so
fast as we suppose.

As I have said, we are engaged in attempting to assess
critically the assumptions of Dr. Doxiadis. The most important of these assumptions concerns the population of the
Great Lakes area in the year 2000. How big will the Great
Lakes megalopolis be? How big will the urban Detroit area
be? We call it Detroit, but, of course, it covers the whole of
the area from Saginaw in the north, or a little farther, to
Toledo and south of it, east beyond Windsor, and west beyond Lansing. The need to rethink the physical framework
in which the population of 2000 will live and work springs
from the population growth. The accurate estimation of
the population growth is highly important.

Dr. Doxiadis and his group of experts have put the population of this area in the year 2000 at about twice the present
figure. It is impossible to say with any confidence whether
this estimate is right or wrong. But economists, with their
sometimes rather pedestrian methods, attempt such checks.

As Dr. Downs has said, it is extremely important to remember that this area is part of an open economy; people
move in and move out. In the Great Lakes region moving
in occurred from 1950 to 1955 when the automobile industry was booming. Moving out took place from 1955 to 1960,
and even later, when the automobile industry was less prosperous. People move towards prosperity, away from depression. There is no guarantee that cities grow. To take an
example from my own country, there are a great many
cities, important, well-known cities such as Manchester,
which were smaller in 1951 than they were in 1911. It is important to estimate probable future earning capacity of the
Detroit area and the gross state product for Michigan, to
guess the future developments of the industries of Michigan and of the automobile industry in particular. There are
enormous problems here, as Dr. Solandt has noted. We

may be on the threshold of a huge change – from the world
of private transportation to the world of faster, but corpo-
rately owned transportation. Our best guess produces
rather smaller figures for the population of the Detroit area
than Dr. Doxiadis uses. Projection is based on present
trends, but can the trends of the Detroit area be changed?
If the automobile industry ceases to grow as rapidly as in
the past (an improbable development), will some other
industry come in and cause even greater expansion? Dr.
Doxiadis' picture of the great Eastern megalopolis reminds
one of the change – one could almost say – miracle that
occurred there. Thirty or forty years ago, as the textile industries moved south, New England seemed to be a decay-
ing, depressed area. Then the introduction of the new,
science-based industries led to a great expansion, so that,
when Dr. Doxiadis projects the Eastern megalopolis into
the Great Lakes megalopolis, he implies a similar transfor-
mation. Will this happen? Will Detroit be a great city, the
commercial capital of the Great Lakes megalopolis? Will it
attract a large proportion of new industries? These are the
questions we are asking ourselves.

How do you set out to work a miracle? Could a great
scientific research centre, attached perhaps to the University of Michigan or to one of the other great university
centres, prove as powerful in attracting and moulding new
industries as MIT has been in the New England megalopolis? These are the questions we must consider and
surely such consideration is no waste of time.

Summary

JACK C. RANSOME

THE EIGHTH ANNUAL SEMINAR on Canadian-American Relations at the University of Windsor, Ontario, November 2–4, 1966, brought together government officials, planners, businessmen, researchers, and academicians to consider the implications and problems of "The International Megalopolis." In the main address, "The Prospect of an International Megalopolis," Dr. C. A. Doxiadis defined and discussed a potential supermetropolitan complex that could grow from the interconnections of existing urban clusters at Detroit–Windsor, Cleveland–Pittsburgh, Toledo, and Chicago.

Dr. Doxiadis mentioned the possibility of an eventual northeastern extension of the megalopolis into Canada and pointed out that the Canadian-American rim of the Great Lakes would become increasingly a focal point of many economic and other activities in the North American continent. He predicted that the Great Lakes megalopolis population would be comparable to that of the mid-Atlantic seaboard of the United States by the end of this century.

Some who attended the seminar did not agree with Dr. Doxiadis' predicted growth rate for the prospective megalopolis. Dr. Anthony Downs stated that large stretches of farmland and other areas of low population density exist within short range of existing metropolitan clusters of North America and that it might be fifty years or more before high densities develop between these clusters. Also, it is clear that the Great Lakes, while acting as excellent transportation connectors between major concentrations of population in the United States and Canada, also provide breathing space between them.

Dr. Doxiadis referred frequently to the Eastern megalopolis of the United States. It might be questioned whether the historical situation of the mid-Atlantic region, involving towns and cities closely tied along an important seacost, is of substantial value as an analogy to the likely development of an inland megalopolis that must connect more widely separated cities and must penetrate international barriers between the United States and Canada.

Participants in the conference agreed with Dr. Doxiadis that the current pace of urbanization in the Great Lakes region is very rapid, that large urban communities are spreading out towards each other, and that urban problems, consequently, become more and more critical. The seminar turned to a number of these economic and political problems, and in the limited time allocated to each, produced excellent discussions on the nature of developing problems and some directions towards their solution.

Special concern was expressed about water pollution in the Great Lakes region. Dr. Harlan H. Hatcher and Professor James P. Hartt referred to Lake Erie as a dying lake because of the extensive accumulation of algae, brought about by ever increasing discharges of nitrates and phosphates from soil fertilizers and from home and industrial sewage. Others of the Great Lakes are being polluted in similar ways but to a lesser degree. The low oxygen content of lake waters and the disposal of chemical wastes into the Great Lakes have sharply reduced the fishery resources of this region. It was suggested that all new sewage treatment plants be secondary treatment plants, and that new and old plants be equipped with facilities to remove the maximum amount of phosphates.

The Honourable John Robarts reported that the Ontario Water Resources Commission consulted in 1965 with more than 600 industries known to be discharging improperly treated wastes. Waste-control schedules were established for each. The Ontario Water Resources Commission, the federal Department of Mines and Technical Surveys, the federal Department of Health and Welfare, and the Fisheries Research Board of Canada are making inventories of various physical, chemical, and bacteriological characteristics of streams and lakes in the Great Lakes Basin.

The per capita demands for water have increased geometrically as the Great Lakes area has become more urbanized. Water pollution has outraced attempts to purify, to reuse, and to conserve water. Some groups in the United States have expressed interest in the diversion of Canadian water southward into the Great Lakes. Mr. Robarts and Mr. Herb Gray, MP, indicated that, although Canada apparently has ample waters now in its northern river basins, it must completely inventory its water resources and estimate its long-term demands before any decision is made regarding diversion.

Dr. Ronald S. Ritchie discussed the fact that international boundaries compound the difficulty of investigating sources of water and air pollution and fixing responsibility for such pollution. In some cases, the sources are well known. For many years the highly industrialized communities of Michigan and Ohio have been primary contributors to the air and water pollution at the western end of Lake Erie. Windsor is the recipient of considerable amounts of smoke and chemical pollutants from Detroit industry, but neither the Canadian nor the United States government seems ready to exert the necessary influence to correct this condition. Both countries now seem to be entering a stage of public awareness of problems aggravated by population concentration and industrialization. Recently, substantial appropriations were voted by the United States Congress for the intensive study of various forms of pollution.

Contributors gave attention to communications and transportation problems in a megalopolis. Dr. O. M. Solandt commented that we are on the verge of another revolution in communications. Better voice and video networks may reduce the need for face-to-face contact in some business and service situations, and thus the need for many trips within or between urban communities. The transportation prospects are less bright. New levels of friction and congestion arise each year in our cities. Mr. Marion Clawson said that the provision of ample freeway capacity at peak periods may be a self-defeating process. As highway capacity is increased, use mounts, and congestion is merely on a larger scale. He deplored the increasing proportion of urban and rural land consumed for transportation functions.

The transportation problems of the megalopolis are the extensions of existing impasses in large metropolitan areas. Street and highway improvements are not keeping pace with the production and use of new vehicles. Various solutions were discussed, including automatic vehicle control, high-speed surface public transportation, and trenched or underground train and other forms of public transportation. There seemed to be a consensus that the developing megalopolis will be characterized by continuing urban sprawl and a proliferation of highways to serve decentralized residential areas. Man will continue to demand the portal-to-portal flexibility of private surface transport. If it is taken underground, we lose the flexibility to travel in many directions and construction costs are much higher than for surface transportation. If we go to the air, or slightly above the surface, we encounter air rights and air traffic conflicts.

As international urbanism spreads in Canada and the United States and a megalopolis becomes more of a reality, what governmental mechanisms are available for joint action on problems arising from greater intercommunication? Are there precedents for co-operative effort between the United States and Canada? Dr. Marvin B. Fast stated that at the lower levels of governmental co-operation there are some precedents to support future joint agreements of state, province, and local units, but most precedents involve single-purpose co-operation, such as the construction of drainage works, production of hydro-electric power, or the acquisition and operation of an international bridge. The United States Constitution empowers a state, with the consent of Congress, to enter into an agreement or compact with a foreign power. Several states have minor agreements with local and provincial units of Canada. However, if state–province agreements were to become too broad in scope, or perhaps too numerous, it is likely that the national governments would suggest that the more formal avenue of treaties be attempted.

Several devices were suggested as feasible for the co-operation of communities within an international urban complex. For example, the state of New York and the government of Canada established about thirty years ago the Fort Erie Public Bridge Authority to acquire and maintain an international bridge. But such arrangements are rare. There have been difficulties in the United States in creating interstate agencies for physical planning, and the problems of establishing intercountry agencies are even greater. Another device for international co-operation at the lower levels of government is the interlocal contracting and joint local enterprise. A community might provide fire protection for an adjacent community across an international boundary, for example, or accept students for a special purpose.

It was suggested by Mr. Walter H. Blucher that effective and realistic urban planning be accomplished at local and regional levels on both sides of the international border.

The voluntary metropolitan area council composed of public officials from several governmental jurisdictions has grown in use in the United States and Canada. These councils are forums for discussion, research, and recommendation only. Some now cut across state boundaries and they could be expanded to include representatives from either side of an international boundary, as between Detroit and Windsor. Since Windsor already is part of what might be classified as an international metropolitan region, should it not fully participate in the council of local governments in Michigan?

Examples of international co-operation at the higher levels of government were discussed by Mr. D. M. Stephens. He suggested that the body of principles set forth in the Boundary Waters Treaty of 1909 between the United States and Canada might be followed by sets of principles pertaining to other international problems. The procedures used by the International Joint Commission established by this treaty could be applied to other commissions. The International Joint Commission can call upon the departmental services of either government, and, at the same time, may appoint an advisory board comprised of specialists from the provinces, states, local governments, or universities of both countries. The IJC is a body that can be used to attack megalopolitan water problems. Further treaties and commissions could be worked out to deal with other specific international urban problems as they arise.

The need for a wide range of special commissions and research studies was evident in the discussion with respect to business and the international boundary. Contrasting viewpoints were expressed as to desirable action by the two countries. Some advocated more economic self-sufficiency for Canada while others emphasized that an impressive degree of integration has in fact occurred across the border and that more economic co-operation is feasible.

Mr. G. R. Heffernan suggested that a future international megalopolis involving the United States and Canada must rationalize industry across the border if these countries are to meet the competition of two highly integrated industrial complexes, one in Western Europe with the advantage of the Common Market, and one in Japan. He noted that the interdependent economies of the United States and Canada are prevented from achieving optimum interchange because of numerous restrictions. Protective tariffs constitute major barriers for most manufactured goods traded between the two countries. A joint United States–Canadian study on an industry-by-industry basis was suggested as a preliminary step towards the reduction or withdrawal of tariffs.

Immigration and entry laws and wage disparities reduce the mobility of labour across the international boundary. However, it is a fact that the greatest exchange of labour, the trading of skills, and the drive for wage parity takes place in those large towns and cities which face across the international line. Within the cores of the incipient international megalopolis, manufacturing plants auxiliary to those across the border are common, and technology and trade goods cross more easily. Large amounts of United States capital have come to Canada, especially to the bigger industrial market towns and to their satellites within a sixty-mile radius.

Truly efficient transportation across the international border is lacking. Business still hopes to develop rail rates between the two countries. There is a lack of co-ordination between the states and provinces, within and between countries, on such matters as highway load limits and highway regulations. A gap exists in the technology of barge movement on the Great Lakes, and handling costs are high at terminal points. The seasonal problem of Great Lakes shipping is still to be solved. Bridge and tunnel tolls and customs inspections are sources of irritation and friction at crossing points, some of which are almost in the centre of the megalopolis. As the interchange of goods and peoples increases, international transport may be forced to improve and restrictions may be relaxed.

For the most part, the seminar participants seemed to accept the premise that a megalopolis is in the making and is more or less inevitable. As Dr. Hatcher indicated, the shift of people from country to town in the Great Lakes region has been relentless. The southern side has long been recognized by social scientists as an impressive transportation corridor and manufacturing belt. The rise of industrial districts on the northern shores of the Great Lakes Basin is the beginning of a complete ring of dense population. Between 1951 and 1961 the metropolitan areas in Canada increased in population by over 60 per cent. The urban population of Canada now comprises 75 per cent of the national population. This growth tends to make a myth of the frontier of Canada. The pronounced migration is southward, not northward.

Increasingly, Canada will encounter the urban problems of the older metropolitan areas of the United States, even though it will have the benefit of their history and their mistakes. Is it necessary to have such monster developments of supermetropolitan regions? Can both countries work towards more decentralized planned towns, screened, at least in part, from the older communities which often appear to be beyond control?

The conference discussions made it quite clear that both short-term and long-term planning, on the local, state–province, and national planes must move forward more rapidly than in the past. If urbanization, industrialization, and pressure on natural resources are to be chronic conditions of the Great Lakes region, then each community must determine its future role within the megalopolis, recognizing that the problems of the whole become the problems of the part.

The conference achieved its objectives. It presented the challenging concepts of Dr. Doxiadis on international urbanism. It re-examined many problems that have confronted Canada and the United States for years, but this time in the context of cumulative and accelerated effects brought about by population concentration. Perhaps the seminar was not able to treat in adequate detail any of the problems discussed, but the participants made manifest the nature of these problems with considerable insight and frankness. It reflected the fact that more and more decision-making groups in both countries are thinking of the future in larger and more co-operative terms. As Dr. Hatcher emphasized, "not only should we have borders without vehemence, but an environment without borders might be worth our efforts."